Fishback Hill

By Dwight R. Droz

Edited by:
   K. D. Kragen
   KaveDragen, Ink.
   kdkragen.com
   Bainbridge Island, Washington, USA

Product design/layout by K. D. Kragen
Cover design by Jerry George
Image scanning/photo editing and restoration
      by Jerry George and K. D. Kragen
Technical Advisor, Don Taylor

Unless otherwise noted, all sketches and
illustrations are by the author, who studied art
with Mr. Neilson at Southern Branch University
in Pocatello, Idaho.

Scandia Patch Press
633 Northwest Scandia Road
Poulsbo, Washington 98370
scandiapatchpress.com
Printed in the U.S.A.
10 9 8 7 6 5 4 3 2 1

Fishback Hill

By Dwight R. Droz

Scandia Patch Press
Poulsbo, Washington

Many a night I saw the Pleiads,
rising thro' the mellow shade,
Glitter like a swarm of fire-flies
tangled in a silver braid.

Alfred, Lord Tennyson
"Locksley Hall" (1842)

Photo/image credits, in order of appearance including page numbers (all images used with permission):

✶ *Alaska State Library, Alaska Historical Collections*: PCA01-1923 (Alaska State Library Core Photograph Collection) *p.10*, PCA125-21 (Alaska State Library J.M. Blankenberg Photograph Collection) *p.11*, PCA297-220 (Alaska State Libray Early Prints of Alaska Photograph Collection) *p.12*, PCA107-21 (Alaska State Library Frank Leslie Baker Photograph Collection, Barley, photographer) *p.13*, PCA297-225 (Alaska State Library Early Prints of Alaska Photograph Collection) *p.15*, PCA87-0682 (Alaska State Library Winter & Pond Photograph Collection) *p.23*, PCA277-1-9 (Alaska State Library Wickersham State Historic Site Photograph Collection, Larss & Duclos, photographers) *p.25*, PCA230-02 (Alaska State Library, Arthur Clarence Pillsbury Photograph Collection) *p.27*, PCA87-0715 (Alaska State Library Winter & Pond Photograph Collection) *p.27*, PCA39-843 (Alaska State Library Winter & Pond Photograph Collection) *p.28*, and PCA297-216 (Alaska State Library Early Prints of Alaska Photograph Collection) *p.32*.

✶ "Dead Horse Trail" (*Hegg 3101*) *p.34*, courtesy of the *University of Washington Libraries, Special Collections*.

✶ *Salem Oregon Public Library, Ben Maxwell Collection*: Photo:7328, Photo:6266, Photo:6259, *pp.105, 106, 113*.

✶ Cover by Jerry George. Cover photo (PCA 277-1-9, "Soapy Smith's Saloon") by Larss & Duclos.

To My Father, Robert Humbert-Droz, Who Climbed The Chilkoot Pass After Gold In 1898 —And To My Horse, Who Didn't

A Tribute to Maude

When I was a young lad on a farm in Idaho
  they worked children hard over ninety years ago;
"Bring wood!" says mom. Pop adds, "Go and hoe!"
Life on our homestead held barrels of woe.

You had to tag a harrow, pitch hay and shuck corn,
  and you don knee-slidin' britches every Sunday morn.
Schoolteachers back then were cranky at school,
  who "whopped" us with rulers to teach the golden rule!

I got a break. The change was broad.
  Herding cows, debonair, on a mare named Maude.
This pony was kind, neat, fleet, and smart;
  we will now interpose a "prosy" part.

"Maudie" minced across our bridge like any circus clown;
  but one day my saddle turned and I'm upside down!
She doesn't bolt, or even move a hair—
  I climb off a-shakin', and pat and pet her right there!

Through all the hard years on our farm I spent,
  Maude was a blessing from Heaven sent.
When I pass on some day, I hope to see
  a red mare in the sky roamin' wild and free!

**Left to right: Dolly, a black pacer, Jiggs, a bay,
and Jiggs' mother, Maude, who ran the corral.**

CONTENTS

Maude

Fishback Hill

By Dwight R. Droz

"Oregon Scene" by Dwight R. Droz

Forward

I often consider the small delights we enjoy in this life on earth to be the most valuable. Plagued with all manner of daily disasters, distresses and trials, humankind longs for respite and refreshment. Sadly, our therapists, healthcare conglomerates and spas-retreats are reaping financial reward from many who have yet to realize there is a simple "balm" to ease the pain of this life, rejuvenate the soul, restore hope.

Not too many years ago, as I wandered unsuccessfully from one purveyor of peace to another, I came upon a gentleman who seemed to possess at least one secret ingredient of the aforementioned "balm." I imagine he discovered it at least in part while wandering around a place called Fishback Hill some eighty-plus years ago. Perhaps *epiphany* is a little dramatic to describe what I wish to relate, but a change came over me as this gentleman shared the benefits of imagination and careful observation of the wonders of both the natural world and the human condition.

As do all of Mr. Droz's writings, *Fishback Hill* illustrates the excitement and variety of our heritage, the comedy and the tragedy of everyday life, the deceptions we often encounter, and the subtle beauty of creation. His prose and poetry melt together in a way that arouses the child in us—in itself a worthwhile diversion from our high-speed, high-tech world.

As a retired naval officer (actually, *sailor* is the more accurate term), I recall a shipmate of Chinese decent who asked me one day, "Hey, let's go get lost." Being a sport, I agreed. Later, I found out that this odd expression of his meant simply "Let's go sightseeing." Anyway, we took off without any real intention except to enjoy the day and experience a foreign land.

Dear reader, I would encourage you even now, if life has handed you some unsavory experiences lately, to take a trip to Fishback Hill and "get lost." It just may be the best way to find yourself.

L. B.
U.S.N., Retired

★★★ Southeast Alaska ★★★
With Skagway, gateway to the Klondike,
at top center of map.

INTRODUCTION

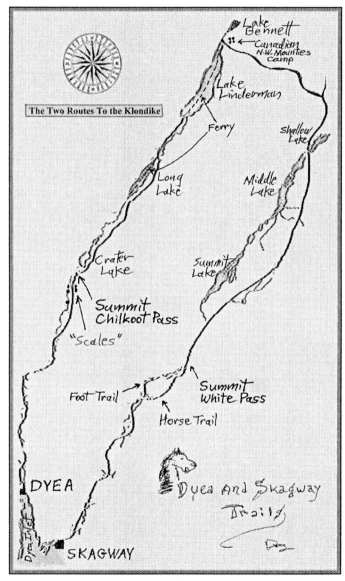

1898: The preferred route to the Klondike, from Dyea's Inlet, was over Chilkoot Pass via "The Scales"; a more hazardous route out of Skagway was over White Pass, traversing what became known as "Dead Horse Trail," eventually littered with the carcasses of over 3,000 pack animals.

Introduction

Dad was in the Klondike in the great Alaska Gold Rush of 1898. A millwright, builder, engineer, to have such a grand adventure at such an early age—what an inspiration he always was to me. His venturesome spirit along with an amazing knowledge of saw and grist mills filled his tales which he spun for me in firelight evenings

I also had a wonderful teacher in college, Florence Jones, who taught me the art of writing and poetics. She never saw any of my work. I've always wondered what she would have thought of it. I've always wished I could have thanked her.

Dwight R. Droz

The Droz Family in St. Anthony, Idaho, 1913. Left to right: sister May, mother Olga, sister Dora, Dwight and father Robert, and either brother Roy or Luke with their dog.

Acknowledgements

Thanks go to cousin Charles Droz and his son Eric who supplied us with the images of our family crest and shield, including wonderful photos of the stained-glass church window with the Humbert-Droz crest in it.

Special thanks to the Alaska State Library Historical Collections archive for many of the photos of the Alaska Gold Rush, Chilkoot Pass, and Soapy Smith; specifically, thank you Mary Anne Slemmons, Library Assistant, Historical Collections, Alaska State Library. Appreciation to Kris Kinsey and the University of Washington Libraries, Special Collections, for the photo of Dead Horse Trail. Thanks also to the Salem Public Library Historic Photograph Collections, the Ben Maxwell Collection, for photos relating to hop farming, the electric ferry on the Willamette River, and the Isis Theater; appreciation especially to Monica Mersinger, Salem OnLine History, Salem Public Library—always helpful.

Finally, much appreciation goes to the wonderful staff of Mitzel's Restaurant, Poulsbo, Washington, who have hosted book signings and graciously displayed and sold many copies of Mr. Droz's books since the launching of Scandia Patch Press ten years ago.

PART ONE

KLONDIKE TALES

Soapy Smith

Soapy Tales Of Alaska Dales

Introduction

Here's a tale I too want to read; this is a story we really need. Based on true cases, it tells what we dream and what fools some are to prate "self esteem." It covers folks I knew so well, and the fantastic tales bold liars tell, smidgens of fancy, grains of truth. Hopes and dreams we shared in our youth; bared in our age at grim 86. Stories amassed by a kid from the sticks. As I write the old clock ticks; so, linger a moment, as we say, no need to push Klondike history away

I won't put you on. I won't put it off. It's a day of computers old timers scoff—a day of awakening, time of content; so put on your glasses; your attention's well spent. I don't cotton to fiction; love fanciful skits, centered on history—with a book in my mitts.

First locomotive in Alaska, Skagway, 1898.

On September 24, 1875 George Holt became the first white man to cross Chilkoot Pass.

Little beginnings—big things to follow.

On August 20, 1896, Skookum Jim showed George Carmack where to find gold down on Rabbit Creek, and all hell broke loose.

Geo. Carmack

The Stroller, an honorable man, formerly known as Esmer White, had a mountain named after him for the stories he would write. After a quarter century of selflessness, he was on his way at the expense of the territorial government in Victoria where he could enter a home for old men and continue the same kind of life.

Once, the Skagway city fathers picked the Stroller to judge a greased pole fray. The other stein of this consign pranced in on a big, white horse; he was Soapy Smith, and up to no good. Well, Soapy only lasted six months on this Skagway scene; a vigilante finally plugged this noxious wolverine.

Jefferson Randolph "Soapy" Smith: perhaps the most well-known person connected with the gold rush, he was an intelligent criminal and controlled a well-organized underworld of thieves, thugs and con-men.

Skagway lay a thousand miles away from law and order and attracted scores of society's outcasts. Smith organized the town's underground criminals for his own nefarious ends.

With so many tales of real life, seems to me even a corpse with oxygen strapped to his bed could rise and devise an opus on facts that I have read. Few histories I've perused could walk the track that Soapy used. Drinking and sinking in a barrel of bellicose blues.

Once I had a friend who told me during tea, she was marooned in an arctic storm on an Autumn morn with snow banking frivolously. This couple had a gun with but one bullet to go—little food, a risky soiree. Another story we plan to tell is how a Swiss miller succumbed and fell, caught in the Klondike's sinister spell. I knew him well; as a babe I played on his knee.

Time passes. The notables of Skagway, the entrepreneurs of Nome, all built their shacks and paid their tax, fell dead or headed home. Most stories began in climes of ease, and ended where *Aurora* weaves above the arctic seas.

Born in Georgia in 1860, Soapy Smith harked from a wealthy family fallen on hard times. He drifted west as a young man, lured to dance halls and gambling dens, hustling and sharking Colorado locals, to finally perfect the con-man's trade. Hearing of the Klondike gold rush, he joined the northward migration.

I remember Wolf Larsen; White Fang was his pup. Old Wolf was "burning daylight" and the bugger wouldn't give up. But I was just a kid, and didn't savvy up. Poet Robert Service is a guy who really earned his pay; and his character Sam McGee remains with me unto this very day!

I like comic strip gags and scalawags, comedians with hype-and-glib; so tuck me in the ol' high chair and hustle up muh bib. I'm still a little kid inside, although I'm 92.

Spin me tales of Skagway raiders hikin' up the Chilkoot's lip. I wanna rush out'a the brush and beg gold for my tip. Even women climbed the gruesome grades—a few, just now and then. But, I tell you, they had courage, more than some gentlemen! So, let's pan gold again!

Workers, dreamers, cheater liars—how dame history conspires—confusing and amusing as Borealis trails her fires. Louse Town roomers, gals in bloomers, maids in overalls. Good men, bad men playing "win or

lose"—intriguing as a "Joseph's-coat" of scintillating hues. This is a trail of tales you may choose to peruse.

The Stroller in December's pall, heard of a crisis where ice-e-ous bulrushes sloppily-sprawl. A bungling moose cut the telegraph line, and a pole fell down in the ancient pine. Town folks love jokes and "news-the-dudes-peruse"; now, your cupboard's de-Hubbered and your kids need shoes! But, hey! It's okay if ya still get some good news! Not today, it's all blues.

The Stroller's a writer who reads your bean, knows your woes and the cracks between. His editor says: "Either quit or cut bait." There's little time to ponder it. Barge out in the gale; don't mind 60 below.

At this point, the Stroller skims his bean and all the crevices between. He flaunts out in the mud and crush navel-deep in rock piles, slush and snow. This *is* an arctic picture show!

By late January, 1898, Soapy Smith was the un-crowned king of the Skagway underworld. Six months later he was gunned down by surveyor Frank Reid on the Juneau Company Wharf in Skagway harbor.

You've got two characters and a deadline scene, so fire up your nicotine; Get out the whiskey, enjoy the play. Cursed by the "Ides of Hudson's Bay"—a mutinous patch of drifters who live in a nasty klatch. There's ol' Soapy, I kid you not, this guy's queasy as a chamber pot. The headlines went something like this: *In wild Skagway, former mobster of the Denver underworld Soapy Smith along with his personal army of three hundred gangsters raped, pillaged and murdered the citizenry indiscriminately.*

Caught outside in icy puddles, the polar-Stroller slows his battle; he knows he's not in Camelot, stuck in a batch of gravel!

A storm is raging on the beach; the ice flows groan and crack. You can see it's rotten weather.

So he types the following, back in the shack: "The Ice Worm Cometh"—my hands and feet are numb, but I made it back to the cabin and I am frazzled, plumb!

Well, he wrote a fantasy story about an ice-worm ball. I'm sure he wouldn't have done it sober, but he had no news at all. Fact was he would have been fired if he hadn't lied it right! It turned out to be a winner; the readers lapped it up. They pinned his opus in the halls, and corridors rang with "How's y'alls!"

I do not fake this story; I print this memo black. Saloonkeepers all over the north thought this was a "National Inquirer" paperback. (Jack London, stuff your scruff in a sack!)

Erudition and cute capers
    work in Brooklyn or Versailles,
But smarts won't git a tinker's nit
    when snow blows twenty feet high!

There's cliffs of it from Chilkoot's mitt,
    and off to the British Isles.
In Iditarod, both bard and lady
    mush flakes a zillion miles.
These folks are tough as iron guff
    you drive in railroad piles.

Soon the saloons sold ice-worm drinks[1]
    and the bartender serves the Stroller free;
They had a lot of fun that day;
    I can hear him say, "I never thought
    they'd name a mountain after me!"

Next, the Stroller pans the "boosters";
    poor spittoon-hounded roosters,
Who swamp the premises each night;
    dump the garbage, maybe mop;

---

[1] Bartenders froze spaghetti (for the worms), and served "ice cube-cocktails" at the bar, garnished with maraschino cherries, what a delightful ploy it war!

They expect these slaves to work non-stop,
   who drain the half-sipped glasses
      unto the final drop.

A sucker arrives, gold in hand;
    eager to draw a spread so grand.
He dreamed of this while grubbin' rocks;
    his tactics thoroughly planned:
"Checkakos, clear the tables;
    boosters git out muh way!
"Good losers, picky boozers,
    pull up a chair and play!
I come outa the mine—um feelin' fine—
    the nickname's Lucky O'Shay!
      So, let's play!"

The Stroller views with pity;
    they need a holiday.
Never enjoy sunlight, men of the night;
    no one knows how to pray!
Crawl under the table, try to sleep.
    One eye open, one orb shut;
It seems useless to practice counting sheep.
    Charles Dickens would pen their fate,
      planning the roles of a reprobate.

The Stroller winced; felt grim remorse;
    wished he'd increased their *tour-de-force*.
Then, he shrugged, "They lack advice:
    union rules could break some ice!"
He herded them under a bay side pier,
    and said, "Boys, we have a quorum here!
I noticed your soup at noon was too thin;
    it's a bad mess you're livin' in.
Sleeping under tables, swamping out the joint,
    ya need to ask new favors;
      do you get the point?

"Is there any new biz?" cries the Stroller;
        every cooster rubs his face.
Says one of the group, "I'm tired uh soup;
        we could of all died with no trace!"
One sad-eyed loner, a simpering groaner,
        peered through thick lenses and said:
"Like once every week, I vote a new tweak—
        make a stab fer a slab uh cream cake!"

"Yeah," howled a buddy, wrinkly and wry.
        "I second!" he yipped as History crept by.
Each Wednesday noon, they now partake.
Weeks after, how they grin
        when the Stroller toddles in.
He's puffing a cigar;
        boosters feel the light.

They're proud for one concession;
        even boostering can be a profession!
So now we close the "Booster News"
        en-captioned as the "Stroller Blues!"
I long for the glow that sparks Sam McGee,
        but he is all mashes in cinders and ashes
                as any historian can see!
Where is Soapy? O, Chute! He's climbing Chilkoot
        neck-deep in "reep" snow-potpourri.
                No joke for the bloke, let him be!

There was a chap, dub him Charley—details
grow dim. The editor slumped in his chair, perturbed
by declining sales. Meanwhile, out in twenty-foot
piles, it's sixty below on trail turnstiles. This is a yarn
of scant repute, but mostly history, so we have to
pursue't.

Meanwhile, in the outback, the evergreens
wrack; icebergs grind as they pile in a pack. It will be
spring a'fore they come un-wacked.

That grim editor boots Charley outa the barn, same as the Stroller in a much better yarn.

As Polar bears nod in the nude
　　deep in the snows of high altitudes,
Poor old Charlie dons his skis,
　　his parka, hood and seal puttees,
And says, "O, m'god! I'm gonna freeze!"
　　Best pull the curtain, times like these.
Lashed to a pack, on a crick in his back,
　　is a jug of Joe Daniel, a frayed writer's manual;
A wedge of moldy limburger cheese;
　　he spots a tepee
　　　　in some trees!

Here an old guide with a beetling brow lets pushy white folks know he won't kowtow.　He meets with Charley; they have a parley—unseparable by now. These chaps so lonely, are full of baloney, get plastered and chew-the-fat.
O, drat!

This underpaid reporter and his Chief-referee this day sashayed a sagacious-page now locked deep in Skag's history, on the day a chief hops outa the hay, to unravel a mystery.

Charley pours a drink as "chiefie" hoists a snort. "That's mighty good stuff," he mumbles, "but this shot glass is short!"　Outside the wind's raging; the tepee's branches shake.　Charlie thinks I need some chummy news as my whole career's at stake!

Chief opines (I can't recoup his brogue, he's a wordy type of rogue): "I remember when my Aleut friend was broke an' outa luck. He climbed a ridge near Dead Horse Pass; huntin' gold with an old spy-glass.
"He swears he seen a boat ! It warn't afloat—"

Charlie's eyes show great surprise.

"In the midnight gloaming," continues Chief, "when wolves are roaming, I've heard tall tales of spooks in the swales when nights are foul and damp." Charley huddles in the shadows, under a smoking lamp. (Men tell such tales when wily winter wails and you're the last geezer in camp.) Finally, Charley responds, "Did'ja ever hear about Noah's ark, a boat with multiple rooms? Story goes: the animals left as a final thunder blast booms. At last it lit on Ararat."

Chief rouses at that; his face holds a trace of a yawn. Says he, "Some missionaries spoke of all this; then, I figgers, by jiggers, those birds messed up. We could never agree very long!

"There's mountain spirits in these hills, the gullies and the draws. Spooks slyly creep under yonder rocks; when late night banshees call. Life up hyaar ain't no Goldilocks bazaar. Shinnyin' up these cliffs ain't no birthday ball!

"All the shamans in our pack—every mother's son guards his back when the lightnin' snaps and rip tides weasel on—and northern lights fire-up nearby. That's the only arc I seen, not for animals millin' round as rainbows rim the weepin' sky. 'Borry Allis' has arcs too!"[2]

A Tepee—
Western Plains
Indians.

About this time, the chief passed out...and maybe will some of you!

---

[2] Of course, a play on words, "arc" versus "ark"; and "Borry Allis," a by-play on the Aurora theme. Now, you decipher with childhood's eyes, mystic bars of light in flaming northern skies as the pole star glimmers white where Sawtooth ridges rise. (I saw 'em once in Idaho, Monday, May 31, 1999.)

The Odd-Couple Club

One chap packs a story, the other serves the dues. Every tale the Indian pitches, he forestalls IOU's. You could say he's on the payroll, a reporter, if you choose. A chap with no diploma, owns three tepees, five wives, an indigenous cuss who hates a fuss. But his wisdom's truly first class. Next morning:

> "So long, Chief," old Charlie calls;
>> as wild winds whip the tepee walls.
> The old sap huddles on th' mattress hay—
>> sleep on, Yo Ho! Anchors Away!

And so, back in Skagway this hit the fan, a headline hyper-quake. In type, for goodness sake:

ARK RE-APPEARS IN KLONDIKE SKY

There are some deviations, historic machinations; but basically, the tale's nearly straight, that latches up one Indian (just an old cheapskate) and a writer, poor old blighter, who does prevaricate. They love to bait news-hungry males and ladies impaled on pitiless trails of the cold Alaskan dales.

Sinister Soap

The crystal image is milky, faintly glow the streets of Skag; holding all the lure and hip-pizzazz of a ten-bar Tiger Rag. Here a man is selling "whatsis," a chap with wan mustache, a slim, trim vest, one wide brim-hat; he's full of pep and dash.

The gold rush ripping on its way infects all folks around. You're farmin' in the middle west, and then... you're Skagway bound. Coming wasn't easy; this is gamble-dogged domain. Folks arrive by horse, then boat, in big boots and overcoat; some bum-ride on a train. The moral is: the West is wide and starts to boom again! A vessel lands on Seattle sands, loaded

with stacks of gold.

Suddenly, you don't mind the strain, buy parkas for cold rain, they stock gold pans and gin. A fool arriving in, views the harbor with a grin intones: "Come on, boys, and count me in! They're pickin' nuggets in the creeks; they're sluicin' through the draws. I'm heading for the Klondike!"

That's really how it was. How do ya think Seattle got so big along the way, old friend? It was the Klondike that built this town to stay.

And when the boom is over and all the rites assay, Seattle's docks and hills and walks reflect Alaska's fateful sway, the lure of Gold, the Western fold and beautiful sights today. Look at Smith Tower, what a sight! The Needle piercing sky, the sound of gulls, old tanker hulls and Ivar Haglund's cry who fed us all on mussels; how he made that guitar fly! Seattle has a special glow with the Olympics gleaming nigh. O, many love the Middle West, the grains like Kansas-sea; but I love Puget best of all! God made it for you and me! The woods and glades; those pretty maids; fir spires high and free.

Don't chop more woods for freeways. Use transit more; and see, that we keep our youth and search for truth—that we have room to be. Lake Washington is such a one; bejeweled with nightly stars, as God looks down upon our town, but why so many cars?

Now, back to my story of Soapy's crush and how this city framed the gigantic Klondike Rush. That was easy rhymin', but we've reached Soapy's domain. And it will be much tougher to unravel all his pain. We don't know much more good about this gink, a gambler-type with cons and hype that drives some men to drink. He combs the Skagway streets, a bag o'bones and sin. Cards are his trade and a green eye-shade; he's eager to

begin. With Lady Luck and a couple of bucks, he'll use his wits to win.

From a battered suitcase came holey socks, some undies in an old black box; he dumped a batch of cheap cigars and plumped in lots of new soap bars. He wrapped them in paper with colored twine. "A'ha!" grunts Soapy. "They're lookin' fine!" That is, thinks he, a seller's line.

He's on a corner of a Skagway street with the case on a stand looking pretty and neat. "There's one bar in here with a five dollar bill! He adds them so folks will get a thrill!

"Yea! It's only a buck for a full sized bar. So come right up! Just the way ya are!" It's a con job geared for miners; but his fame spreads pretty far. "Try a sample," Soapy cries, trying to man a grin. "They smell as rich as roses, and they're easy on the skin!"

By Droz

Soapy Smith
&
—An Impression—

"Soapy's my name; remember it well!"
Most miners did; a truism from Hell!

And this is how he started, as I my crystal skim, the images are stark, but I'm very sure of him. Here appear the streets of Skagway, men from Dyea's tidal mat; where they dump all steamer cargo; some, in twenty minutes flat. You're ultimately lucky if the tide is coming in. On the other hand, you could be shocked if belongings try to swim. It all depends on time and tide when you spot-land on Dyea. That happened to a lot of men who didn't know the way. Mud flats are a poor excuse; so travelers who didn't know the ropes wound up a silly goose.

Everything about the Klondike jaunt is subject to reproof; as bad as if you fill a house before you mend the roof. Speaking of Seattle, home of the merchant fleet; the gold strike in Alaska knocked the town right

off its feet. The fishermen and lumber-jacks and sailors
from the sea. All climbed aboard a steamer and headed
for 'Duryee'. Those bearded, booted miner types set out
with rosy cheeks. It will be a year, you little 'schmeer',
before you mine the creeks. The ice, wild rides, rivers
and tides, swift rapids and mud flats. There is enough
to call your bluff and drive chekacko's bats. In fiction
you plan an ending. In real life, brace your feet; so just
enjoy some *deja-vue*, the French say it so neat.

Time passes; Soapy runs a saloon, becomes the
poor man's host. He plays a role of Samaritan, just like
Rasputin's ghost. He gives good vibes and pays thieves
bribes; hands out money for any cause, but the bitter
truth is he's uncouth and breaks all city laws. And the
forty-niner who gets caught up in his claws.

Yes, Soapy's generous, and tenuous; but
underneath he's marred. And so's his role in history, a
scurrilous petard. And yes, his fate's ill-starred. He had
some fatherly interests. Colorado was once his home.
But when he gets in a lather, he's as full of hot air as
foam. Did he miss his wife and children; did their
absence cause him pain? Soapy is a villain, and that
report is plain. Vigilantes were on his trail, but he ran a
wide campaign. What was his greatest heyday? It was
on a fourth of July; Soapy gathered all the goops, the
barkeeps from his sty. Boosters who sleep under tables,
working for soup-and-rye. The guys who swab
spittoons on scatter sawdust day, a bit of gruel, a game
of pool and scraps that come their way.

He mustered up a big parade, a Chamber of
Commerce Show. Town fathers looked down upon that
crowd, but they livened streets below. A ragtag of
oopsy-doos, the nerds, the bums; thieves brigands, like
rolling bands, and folks with brains half-numb.

Good citizens got "wopped" into very odd

terrain. After all, Independence day is no place for 'Chataquaine'. Soapy rode a big white horse, the head who ran the force; this was a happy train. So that ragged rout was awed when a tuba O-o-m!-pa!-pahd!

> They're banging drums up First and Main,
> Another John Philip Sousa'n-type refrain.

When the parade was over, he'd spent a little dough; but now comes the reckoning, a facet of the show. You know when entertainment stops; when you drink and lick the spoon; the only place on earth for a brawl like this was

SOAPY SMITH'S SALOON!

Now others gained some shekels; some 'merchies' sold butcher knives; but most of the dough in 'Skag-a-mo' wound up in Soap's archives. A few good deeds he mustered—floss the riddle of his life—news that he had children, a long-neglected wife.

Dear God! Skagway streets were cold! One Soapy fact is he stole, intact; there was fate in the dice he rolled. Suspicion is he caused miners to die because he needed gold.

Like a roving spider, he sets his web; sinister, seldom a smile. A grim 'arachnidian' grimace contains his brief profile. Too grim to laugh, hard to photograph, there's little to compile.

But one thing I must tell you. It struck me as quite strange; he was put on a committee with the Stroller, a tweak-up for a change. City fathers coupled them for a greased-pole ride, and so their paths collide. They carved a stone for the Stroller. They named a mount for Soap. They buried one reporter with honor; and the bartender molds on the slope. The saloonkeeper died a big "conner":

> For he was a goner, a dope.
> And if it were a play,
> You could end it this way;
> "Wreathed with a necktie of rope!"[3]

In this battered grip, lie tiers of soap wrapped in scintillating foil.

"Step right up, gentlemen. Here's the finest stuff in Skag, protects from gleet and tired feet! And I don't mean to brag. Ya may even find a five dollar bill, I put in some to make a kill."

Now and then, one henchmen steps up to buy a bar. The price is only a dollar. That seems quite *far and squar*. (When yer mug's full-a-chawtabacca, that's how the diction war).

Soapy's saloon entertains misfits—like jackals they roam the veldt—men who love gold bits are quick of wits with a pistol on their belt. A thirty-eight year old gambler, he'd no Colorado fame. Soap sales earned him consternation and sparked his odd nickname.

---

[3] This line of rhyme is a bit of poetic whimsy—there being a story circulating about that Soapy was hung by the Mounties—which in fact is untrue. Soapy was shot by Frank Reid in a duel, 8 July 1898.

Let's move on to a famous point known as Chilkoot Pass, bounded by Canada and Alaska, a tract as slick as glass. Mounties planned to man the border, chose a slope where rose "the Scales."

A staging ground, a shelter shot up of rocks, tents and "krup," all things were helter-skelter at first.

In no time at all they had scales at this mall, because the mad Klondike had burst. They brought

weighing scales to check tall tales. Those officers went right to work.

Miners climbing the height, couldn't travel too light. Six months worth of food was one perk. They weighed all gear of the tenderfeet here. No one should steal or intrude. All criminals barred, the scales were a yard on a slope where supplies were reviewed. Here miners pitched packs. Then they loaded up their backs and headed for hell up on the slope. That's how men learn to cope.

In a little valley, that was the last staging area before stampeders went "over the top," men rounded up their packs and prepared for the final ascent of the mountain: a grade of thirty degrees up some twelve hundred steps gouged in the frozen snow.

"The Scales" got it's name from the Indian guides who weighed their packs here on a primitive balance before starting up.

Here is a singularly entertaining portrait of Soapy Smith and his gang from the Case and Draper

Collection of the Alaska State Library Archives. Soapy is the fourth man from the right.[4] The chap to Soapy's right reminds me of Charley Chaplin, the "little tramp," hat and all. Soapy Smith's true name was Jefferson Randolph Smith (1860-1898), but he was nicknamed Soapy when he began selling soap on street corners for one dollar a bar, wrapping one five dollar bill around one soap bar as a reward.

Soapy was one known gambler and a huckster who would not be allowed to climb Chilkoot Pass. Soapy, no-doubt, didn't want that privilege anyhow. He chose to dig his gold dust at his Skagway saloon. So what did Soapy do? He enlisted the aid of a character actor of great spirit and many gifts of insight who called himself the "Preacher." He could pray like a demon, sermonize at trail-side funerals, comfort the living and ever declare undying love of his fellowman. When the preacher spotted a miner heading for civilization with a happy face, he took him under his wing.

"Be careful!" he would exhort the pilgrim. "There are men, unlike me," says he, shaking a broad finger, "who will be on the lookout for chaps like you." So these trusting souls were won over and he dutifully accompanied them back to Skagway. Eventually, they wind up at Soapy's saloon where he buys the drinks.

Now, Soapy had a rare bird upstairs; and this is where the plot thickens. "Come upstairs and see the parrot," says the kindly preacher. A few chaps in Soapy's saloon recognize the evil refrain. Point is, another wayfarer, after being wined and dined below, is further entertained on the upper floor—and eventually is dumped in the bay, accompanied by a sack of rocks well fastened—and so it goes. Soapy carefully puts the

---

[4] Note: there is some question whether the individual portraited in this photograph really is Soapy Smith.

stranger's money in his safe. Now, it could be returned in the morn…if his ghost is up to claiming the body.

Too bad! Few patrons revived from specific nights of revelry if they had no friends with them and "the poke" was very fat. This refrain is mindful of an old English ballad of *Jack the Ripper.* He gave haircuts to seafarers with no buddies either.

So how did they disappear? With a lever, a trapdoor, and their faces wrapped in a towel. Now ain't that foul?

In the basement below there was a very unhappy relative of the lady in charge of a restaurant famous for meat pies. Dray men and shopkeepers of London loved to go there. The apprentice had a rather irksome job, it appears; he single-handedly had to prepare the "newcomer" with proper respect and decorum, and grind him for the morrow—a rather boring job, I suspect. The portly cook, well decked in cook's hat and starched accouterments served eager gourmets.

"What grand meat pies!" one and all proclaim. Now, back to the Klondike; and we'll resume our placid tale in view of opera goers.

Robert Humbert-Droz Enters The Scene

I look at a motley group of miners in old photographs, wondering if my father's picture is there. It is impossible to make him out. Odds are against it; nevertheless, Robert Humbert-Droz, a Swiss miller, emigrated from Neuchatel, Switzerland to Neuchatel, Kansas. That I know is correct. Then he got the urge to come to Seattle and follow the golden trail.

I have written this piece because my father told me in his Swiss-brogue that he and two partners had clambered over Chilkoot. They'd engaged an Indian guide and dog team to carry supplies. He'd caught gold fever. Men going over Chilkoot ignored indigents; the sturdiest just went around them, paying little attention to others needs. That was gold fever—a true malady.

Father did find gold and staked a claim; but alas, on returning in better weather at a later time, he could never find the spot. The two who had been partners in the project were never located either. The assay office report acknowledged some gold was in prospect. I regret to say there is no further record I can find.

Here are some highlights of that mad gold rush my father ventured into. George Carmack, Skookum Jim and Dawson Charlie struck gold in 1896 at Rabbit Creek, then renamed Bonanza. But getting there was half the battle. "Stampeders" trekked over treacherous Chilkoot with a required year of supplies—800 kg. or 1,760 lbs. Arriving at Bennett Lake, they cut trees, built boats and waited out the winter. As soon as the ice broke, they set sail for Dawson, running down the Yukon, a fast flowing river notorious for nasty rapids.

That special bivouac, at the foot of Chilkoot's gargantuan grade, consisting of steps, chiseled out of snow and ice, marked the beginning of a trial taxing flesh and spirit. The resolute made it; the maimed, weary and sick often died on the climb.

　　　When dad lit his ever-recalcitrant pipe in our granary, years later back in Idaho, and talked about his search for "gold and grit" climbing the Chilkoot, that ordeal stirred my curiosity.　Was pop exaggerating? We spoke little of it as I grew older.　Now, it comes to full glare in my mind.

　　　The pictures of a long string of miners striving to conquer snow, hunger, strain and grim doubt almost blows my mind.　It was a 30 degree grade!　Miners striving for the summit, left all their possessions at "the scales."　They singled out some 100 or so pounds.　One famous Indian packer carried 165 pounds up that

incline. The vicissitudes of this grade made that near-impossible for most climbers.

Oh yes, you could hire a packer, but the cost was tremendous. So the average miner made seemingly countless ascents and descents of Chilkoot's 1200 steps. How many trips do you think you'd encounter on that staircase?

Sure, there were other methods, like dragging a sled, but that, too, is a grim, dire grind.

Another pass adjoins the Chilkoot to the east, known as White Pass. This was a longer way but mules and horses were often employed on this grade, a place of extreme tragedy. Horses commonly died here. The terrain was treacherous; horses weakened and stumbled by the thousands (by some counts, over 3,000 froze to death), their bones forming part of the trail. Summer brought the stench of rotting horseflesh; blowflies covered everything in a black shroud.

Horses really had no business making the Klondike climb. History proved this over and over. Hay and grain were an imperative need. Feed was in short supply. Soon it was gone. What lay ahead? Starvation. They pushed the mules, mercilessly on White Pass runs; those that fell, due to exhaustion and hunger, were heaved into the canyon below where they writhed, blundered, froze and left marker bones after being devoured by ravens and wolves.

Canadian Mounties commonly patrolled the scales. They were in charge of commerce at the forking of two trails. The Mounties were on the lookout for malingerers near and far. They also protected miners gear while they headed "summitar."

Why did Mounties sneak about? Where do the boundaries lie? Both Canada and USA tried hard to cut the pie. Nobody had a fig-of-fact where national lines overlay. Folks asked for rules concerning mules,

downsized by ricochet; forty-niners, to a man, thought somebody should pay. That's why one Jounty-Mountie, with secretive intent, rappelled to the critters; then, back to bed he went. A sample-case of terrors—errors that harass—his shots rang true, and none to rue location of the ass. Now, a marker spaced in proper place, crowns slopes of Dead Horse Pass.

At the base of treacherous Chilkoot Pass, North West Mounted Police officer Sam Steele described the scene: "Neither law or order prevailed, honest persons had no protection from the gang of rascals who plied their nefarious trade. Might was right; murder, robbery and petty theft were common occurrences."

The alternative White Pass, to the east, was soon dubbed Dead Horse Trail, characterized by the stench of rotting horses which were strewn across it for miles.

"Dead Horse Trail" (University of Washington Libraries, Special Collections, Hegg 3101).

Many men lost their minds on the Dead Horse Trail. Others lost their lives as a diet of rotten horse flesh led to raging fever. Screams of pain echoed through the canyons like dead spirits throughout the winter of 1897.

Overland and river routes from Edmonton were advertised by the city's leading businessmen and politicians as the fastest trip to Dawson; but these "short-cuts" could take up to three grueling years.

Hundreds who left from Edmonton drowned in the mighty Mackenzie River or were frozen solid in the Arctic winter.

To set out as a stampeder during the Klondike Gold Rush of 1897-98 was indeed to risk death on the routes.

Humbert-Droz Coat of arms,
circa 18th century.

The Humbert-Droz Family Line

I received a long letter from Nola Waite, Pauline's youngest sister, who compiled an extensive genealogical record of the Waite family. Nola married John Waite. His family are Mormons. Almost all Mormons are vitally interested in family trees.

I always enjoy Nola's letters. Nevertheless, I am blandly envious of their sense of history and the way they check the archives to gain every crumb, collecting past achievements. So, I decided it was moot to mention some Droz family history, and to recognize our achievements after arriving in America. I desired to boast a bit of our own family escapades and background, friend or foe. What follows is a report of our Swiss roots.

My daughter, Deanna, married Donald Thomé, a retired Naval Commander. He was the only son of a Finnish family who, like my parents, emigrated to America from Europe. Those remnants of our ancestors—those guarding, ghostly faces, like the bodiless sprites of old Mt. Rushmore—stare down at me as I write.

Here, in Puget Sound, Washington, I receive emanations of Norwegian flavor each time I drive to Poulsbo. There, we unroll a pleasing-some scroll of Swedes, Danes, Norwegians and Finns, their fetes, sates and sins, in a quaint harbor; there a church spire with loquacious bells informs all comers of "Curfews and dawning's in shops with pleasant awnings."

What an agreeable scene it is. And with that prelude, we gladly enfold Finnish Thomés in these historic musings, our granddaughters and grandsons of note. We acknowledge, as well, the Werder line conjoined with our son, Dennis, and his forthright family who dwell in the environs of seething Seattle.

Our Swiss connections are strong indeed. One ancestor was Numa Droz, a past president of Switzerland.

At this point I wish to underline *one* specific error (or omission) in every genealogical study of my family I have seen. Our name is not simply "Droz." If I were living in Switzerland, I'd be compelled to list my full name as Dwight Robert "Humbert-Droz."

When my father came to America in the 1870s, he was duly processed into the country when Ellis Island was just a Civil War weapons depot. Perhaps his name was "mauled" by clerks, or mayhaps dad decided to clip his name to make it simple as possible. If so, by that thoughtless act, he severed important ties with our Swiss relatives in Europe. Our name has a genealogical breach-of-linkage between Europe and America. Genealogical treatises I receive from Droz publications in the US never find the thread that connects American families with the Humbert-Droz folks in Europe. All reports covering Drozs in America are incomplete. The "Humbert" part is obscured.

Historians are quick to attest many Drozs fought in the civil war. Did you know one bulletin they sent confirmed that my mother, nee Olga Descombés, was the oldest Droz who ever lived on the entire earth? They made a big event of that. But they should have listed her as Olga Humbert-Droz: Dad's name was Humbert-Droz when they married in Switzerland.

(Enough of that; by now, you may see this record is confusing. Many Drozs do not possess the Humbert part; call them cousins, if you will.)

Not one of those genealogies I've perused ever combed the dark secrets of our family to discover the correct name is: "Humbert-Droz." That's right. They simply term us as Droz. Aberrations in names are common in my family.

Here's another: My son-in-law was a Naval Optometrist. In Finland his family name was plain Thome. As years conspired, the French symbol "é" was inserted. Best I can deduce, this was a time in Europe when French accouterments, like "è, é, ê, and ë," struck the fancy of linguists. I guess you could say it was "Tony" at that time. So they changed their name to Thomé. They weren't French, but the name gained a distinct flourish; and so it remains today. Deanna's husband and family are proud of their Finnish roots, amplified by a fancily-bound volume of *luminous* ancestors.

So, you see, Nola, and all relatives on land and sea, the Thomés and the Humbert-Drozs have happy memories of roots, too—as the Werders and the Waites do.

We continually search for Humbert-Droz clues (and few ever appear). Hey, there are scads of Drozs in Switzerland and America. Somehow, they get all the attention of archivists. So that is why we write this tome.

Though they all are related, only *one* family line received a *grant* of land. You may call this a "tall tale," or you may say, "I know Dwight prevaricates!"—or "What a goofy-gaffé?" We will understand.

My granddaughter Gina's husband, Jason Remer, is a gentlemanly chap, but he may concur. Jason runs a nuclear reactor not far away from home that "perks" just like his coffee every morning. He's a nuclear-bound Electrical Engineer. I suspect Jason (a

good friend) shushes, or blandly *poo-poo's* our Northern states foibles. I'll just grin if he's skeptical.

Here's the best way to explain *why* I enjoy the story. My brother, Luke, visited our family home in Lignierés, canton of Neuchatél. There he met Adolphe (or Adoph?) Humbert-Droz, one uncle (a few times removed), alive and ticking, with that "humpish" Droz nose intact. Yes, Adolphe, inherited the selfsame spot where my pop spent his ladly years in a capacious house with many rooms. Luke toured the famous mill, flanked by a flowing stream as the mill-race sparkled with historic jest. My brother remembered dad's boyhood tales; it was true the old mill turned just the way it did when Robert Humbert-Droz (he had no middle name) sawed lumber and ground grain.

> Down by the old mill stream—
> Gurgling sedge and cresses gleam.
> Yellow-caped, a meadowlark
> Chimes hours before and until dark
> Of centuries briefer than we deem!
>
> Alpen summits gleaming where
> Icy peaks in pale hues glow!
> I dream of ancient beauty there
> Amid the high-capped fields of snow—
> A heritage we'll never know!

During his apprenticeship, my father learned several skills: first, as a millwright, a man who builds and services sawmills; next, a timber sawyer. In that capacity, he rode the logs as they approached the saw. Sometimes he nearly fell asleep as the timber neared *the blade*. He had to leap off in a jig and return the sawyer's carriage to the back end of the mill for another pass. He repeated this precarious ride until the log was kaput. It appears the milling process could be altered

so *one man* could operate it in a pinch.

I remember how dad described those late-night ordeals. My mother, Olga Descombés, a Swiss classmate, often mentioned how my father-to-be sometimes dozed over his lesson book at school, after working late in grandfather's mill. There was a firm bond between Olga and Robert—same age, same town, same teacher.

Boys, in those days, rapidly transmuted to men. Every Swiss of sound body and mind was conscripted for the Swiss army. Each candidate was required to bivouac in the Alps, sometime each year, on snow-laden army maneuvers. Every sound, able bodied, soul could be mobilized on the instant in time of war. That was the Swiss strength—the hot spirit—each soldier's gun was kept oiled-and-ready in a secure, back-room closet. I believe that's still true today!

Pardon, if I digress. Beside soldiering skills— on skis yet!—dad learned to repair mill machinery right in his own yard. During my Idaho boyhood, in winter, when farming was slack, he often traveled to Portland or Vancouver installing machinery in sawmills. When he came to America, he was placed in charge of a Roller Mill in Kansas.

Railroad yards and steam roller mills, Centralia, Kansas, where author was born, 1912.

It was a large plant, with a rail yard added to accommodate shipping and receiving grain; grain production was a big industry in Kansas then. Dad would have had an easy life as a miller, doing what he loved to do, but he developed industrial-asthma due to long exposure to mill dust!

He quit milling grain forever, doctor's orders, and coughed constantly the rest of 65 years. What a price we pay for the unpredictable tasks parenting may require!

His father (my grandfather), a redoubtable miller, was a builder as well. He supervised others, building Swiss chalets from the lumber he cut in his own fabulous mill. Some folks get all the gravy, along with the corn. It sounds as if I'm bragging, but I have to report this. I heard it so often. He was the strongest man in the entire village. Why not tuck him in a niche of your family line? He'll fit there just fine!

The fable, so oft repeated states my grand-dad fell from a high scaffold, when building a Swiss chalet. That drastic fall, historians affirm, would have killed lesser men. It drove a stake of wood through his left side. Awed workers gathered him up, sliver and all, placed him on a stretcher and transported him to the nearest hospital. That trip was cumbersome, an ordeal for all concerned. On arriving at the hospital, the stake was perilously removed—grandfather fought to live and won!

He was amazed to be alive. Almost a year after the accident, my grandpop, convalescing, resumed a daily walk down a street adjacent to the mill. On this early trip, he spied two neighbors struggling on the scaffold of a new church steeple. Those men had limited footing; he watched them try to hang the bell, called to inquire what the trouble was.

Answer came back: "We'll have to remodel the scaffold!" one of them yelled.

"Descendez!   Descendez!   Mes   amis!" grandfather called; a group of onlookers gathered nearby. These builders knew one another's abilities well. The two workmen descended without hesitation.

I heard this account many times. My granddad climbed the ladder unaided, braced his feet firmly on the scaffold, seized the bell, and singly and alone, hung it properly—and forever. This episode requires no further glue. My father always contended his kin was a remarkable man.

As for Robert Humbert-Droz, my pop, though we farmed many acres of Idaho soil, some good, some steep or marshy, his main support came from building balloon barns, plain barns, and homes. He renovated and remodeled the first store for Mr. Skaggs, *head of the Safeway chain*, in American Falls, Idaho. (I wrote a tale about dad's early friendship with Mr. Skaggs.) Yes, I knew him, too. We even dined at the Skaggs home in Burley on their invite. I was there.

One reason the Skaggs were good friends was because my mom, an obstetrician, brought little Dwight Skaggs into the world. Mrs. Skaggs bore that child on the Cotterel homestead—my sisters remembered that.

By the way, Dwight stole my name—bad shenanigans occur some times, out there in dry lands. My sisters claim he was named after me. Or to honor mother in some way. Go ahead and laugh. I played with him in later years, on that day we dined with them. Yes, I knew them.

As for me, besides writing, dad taught me to shingle roofs in the twenties.

Looking back, my dad—an unusual man—put up with many physical problems, like asthma, with no

complaint. There was always food on the table. We endured hard times and bank failures like most settling Americans. He was caught in the dry land rush to homestead around Cotterel, along with other farmers like the Schrenks, Kessingers, Skaggs and Vosburgs (in the general area). We nearly starved on that dry land fiasco. After clearing 300-plus acres, all that pain and sweat, we jettisoned in panic, leaving newly-built houses to blister in the sun with doors staved-in and windows shattered by vandals. Many settlers had the same experience.

A Change Of Scene

My parents told this tale many times as we poked sage boughs in the Royal Oak's maw on a rousty winter's night on the Southern Idaho prairie. The story goes thus. Once I had a great-uncle, in Switzerland, the first member of a new clan. He was the one who "'birthed" the Humbert-Droz line.

This legendary fellow formed a group of vigilant-volunteers in the long ago days of warring clans. I must dub in some of the theme, by right of poetic license, let us say. I think the days of swords and crossbows make a fine back drop. (Perhaps history will prove me wrong.) Armed with such weapons—can you imagine the group?—swords and crossbows at the ready, shunning the fireside to launch a social mission, climbing crags and crevasses of a formidable cliff. This was a *life and death* encounter, you see.

All right! I know I seem bombastic. But I'm exhuming a myth of a relative whose name I bear, bringing him to life after dozing for generations under the cold stones of an Alpine graveyard, unsung and unknown.

Our subject is one clan of burly brigands in a classic castle on a pass. This is a true tale. Trust me!

Why weren't these devils on the cliff-top vanquished?
Easy. This clan of mealy knaves were formidable foes
in the early days. Imagine a turreted castle bathed in
snow, like some tale of *Lorna Doone*. There was no
established military presence at that early time.

> Robber-brigands, historians attest,
> Preyed on travelers at the crest.
> No one to protect you, wolves at your back,
> A sharp sword may be all you pack!
>
> Safety's slim; danger's wide.
> At every bend thieves crave your hide!
> Incoming bowmen's eyes are keen;
> The entire scene's a grim machine!
> What's the motive, who gets the purse?
> Who will gain? Who'll be worse?
> So long uncle; so long lad!
> The finest vision any poet had!
>
> Grandees came through—powdered and shaven.
> Rich dukes, frugally charged,
> Thought passage a haven.
> Well-armed folks paid happily for bed and sup—
> Unknown or alone, you may not wake up!
> In a ravine, ravens pick the bones clean—
> The final facet of a killing machine!
> Tinker's cross with a slight coin-toss.
> Beggars may seem unseen—
> Their purse too mean—End of scene!

     Back to the wet, chilled climbers, the foe's a
brutal sort. Who wants being caught-and-quartered in a
risk of *last resort*?

> Brigands post no guards;
> It is a Christmas night.
> Revelers are drinking hard;

There's not a spy in sight—
Not on this night!

This is the crux of the story;
This is the meat of our tale,
Weary climbers, sheets of ice,
Hands grown frozen and frail.
Ropes cut your cheek;
No mystique—a scourge of driving hail.

Loud clamor marks the castle,
It writhes like scythes—a-slope.
The lot of a few invaders
Seems to promise scanty hope!
Is the feat ill-starred? The snow drives hard!
Only fools duel such a night!

Crossbows at ready—
Cudgels in hand—
Can so few men corral a large band?
Could they win? Was the climb ill planned?
There was music and revelry in the halls below.
Not a soul kept guard in this driving snow!

Those weary Alpinists thread the crags;
They climb formidable walls—
With ropes-and-hope, rappel the slopes,
And invade impossible halls!
For curtain calls!
The castle's rammed with contraband,
Fiefdoms beyond belief—
         and now…
It's time to corral the thief!

It's impossible, at this point of time,
To declare how the feat was done;
Hardly a reveler was sober that night;

They subdued every one.
The High Sheriff came at noon next day
from a note posted on his door.
"Come, get our bodies," it might have said,
"If we die in the fray,
Remember us—heretofore!"

Full many prisoners, he carried home—
Wild men sealed in stocks—
So we leave this bastion in disarray,
The huge doors barred with locks...
        for future talks.

As the poem declares, those miserable thieves
were drinking and celebrating as my ancient, grand-
uncle:

Climbed the crags and scaled the walls
As 'round the raging blizzard falls.
Victory was easy. Brigands in jail
Is summation of this tale.
Eventually, I deduce,
Each mother's son died by the noose!

"Ah yes," you'll say, "it's a Grimm fairy tale!"
But, I affirm, history will prevail.
There's *some* truth inside the tale.

Brother Luke viewed the mill in old Lignierés,
Like times when our dad climbed the stairs.
Big wheels turning—grinding flour;
An ancient clock describes the hour—
A heath beneath him thrummed with power!

Luke's relatives located the "coat of arms" in
the stained glass window of a church in Lignierés. I
think that is the right city. It was placed there in honor
of the episode in the poem to respect the Humbert-Droz

family. He brought me a picture; I have it somewhere. Can't lay a hand on it tonight, as I write.

No matter, that church hasn't moved in centuries, but I'll move on soon enough. I told my neighbor, Larry B., that this tale sounds like a replay of "King Arthur," a warrior knighted receives a coat of arms and a grant of land; he grinned and casually asked, "Did they have Kings in Switzerland?"

"I don't know," I truthfully opined. "Someone rewarded a leader for valor. That is what my parents claimed." We leave it thus!

Church of Valangin, Lignierés, Switzerland.

Portion of stained-glass window, church of Valangin.

Full stained-glass window, church of Valangin.

The final part of this story of knighthood granted our clan has many choking morsels for "incoming" relatives to ponder. I'll admit, when you marry into a family, tales like this are hard to *chaw and swallow.*

> So, worthy kin in the old Swiss bin,
> Happily gaze as a rollicking stream
> Plunges to meld a mill-wheel-theme;
> That is how it's always been.
> It joyfully turned every day of our life;
> It spins for my son, my girls—my wife.
>
> Thus, the Humbert-Droz line
> Was honored to be,
> Free of property taxes, states the decree.
> That old tale's good enough for me!

At this juncture, mother added this note: "As years went by and memories dimmed, one bureaucrat incorrectly sent a tax bill. (Remember the mill was tax-free.) A family member, hazy about our history, began paying taxes. An old *vielliard* objected, 'This land was granted us free of taxes forever!' A search was initiated. Payments ended there."

One of our relatives in Arkansas chuckles at this interlude. I have this comment:

> Well, if it isn't so, why does the mill so merrily go?
> And a "coat of arms" basks in the chapel's glow.
>
> Facts-or-fictions love a frivolous course!
> (Like putting carts ahead of a horse.)
> To Humbert-Drozs 'neath Alpine skies,
> Or knights unknown, I bid good-byes.
> Father played Santa on his sled
> As the joyous hours fled.
> Before our Christmas rites were said,

Gifts of holly trimmed the tree
In far off isles of revelry.
Please bring those Noels back to me!

I don't believe in fairies.
I *do* believe in God.
My folks chose Kansas prairies
To blend me with the sod—
I never thought it odd.

Yes, that's the spot where I was born—
A twinkle in my eye.
Mom put it there; dad was most rare;
He joked better than I—
So, would we need to lie?
Take or reject the story; it's much too good to die!

The knight's second blessing was: a gift of land
with a viable stream, granted the family, free of cost—
and tax free, in perpetuity.

In due time, a comfortable house and sawmill
were erected. My grandfather inherited the mill. That's
where dad learned the milling trade. He ground corn by
day; sawed lumber at night. There was a shortage of
new land in Europe.

A depression developed. My father, trapped in
a large family couldn't inherit a dime; so, like hosts of
others, dad emigrated to America. Then he bee-lined
for a small prairie town named Neuchatel, Kansas,
where many Swiss immigrants lived. It so happens
there is a Neuchatel, Switzerland, a district or *canton* in
which is situated the town of Lignierès. So round it
goes!

Coincidences that shape events,
Do mold our lives and our intents.

My deceased brother, Luke, fought in the "Battle Of The Bulge"; shrapnel pierced his back, shoulder and one arm. When he woke from a coma, German voices sounded outside his tent. My God! he thought, I'm not only wounded, I'm a prisoner as well! He passed out again. Things moved rapidly in the bulge. This time he heard friendly, familiar voices. American forces had retaken the ground they'd lost during the night.

After recovering in a Belgium hospital, Luke booked a trip to Switzerland, heading for Lignierés. Soon, great uncle, Adolph Humbert-Droz led him around the site. The mill wheel merrily whirled. The historic house, was still majestic and sound despite the onslaught of centuries—and it is still in the Humbert-Droz family.

Flag of Canton Neuchatel, Switzerland, with green, white, and red panels.

HUMBERT-DROZ

PART TWO

OTHER TRAILS

"Steven's Farm, Forest Grove, Oregon" by Dwight R. Droz

September Song

There's something in September,
      especially at morn,
Like lazy-daisy rhythms
      and tassels on the corn.

The meadow has a halo
      the blackbirds soar in flocks,
And the hazy, lazy river
      circles wheatfields all in shock.

The moon glows round and brilliant,
      the meadow's in a haze,
The apples lie in bushels,
      O, what lack-a-daisal days.

I dream August and September
      are like sisters Siamese,
And only God could render
      two such lovely twins as these.

A Winter Dream

I.

Come, linger by the roaring fire
    where the burnished kettles gleam,
And let the night and storm conspire
    to weave a winter's dream.

The apple sticks burn brightly
    all green and blue they glow
As snowflakes whisper softly
    upon the fields below.

The wind, at times, in flurried gust,
    raps the sill with angry moan;
Its touch is like a rapier's thrust
    that cuts to marrow-bones.

The old clock speaks of suns and showers
    that blend like wind and snow.
Its quavering chimes still mark the hours
    as in the long ago.

A ringing axe! The roll of drums!
    The sound of fife and fair!
A cry of hounds across the wood
    in autumn's smoky air.

Where did they go, those wondrous days,
    the playmates, flown afar?
Cold rime upon the casement prays—
    black night blots the star.

Here, etched in yellow lamplight,
    the dog who guards my door
Mulls old regrets of lost delight
    he shared with sires of yore;

They roamed the whispering poplar,
  they leapt the ringing rill,
And raided the moonbeamed arbor
  that dreams on yonder hill.

Pomona loved this leafy wood
  where cloistered aspen climb—
And many's the lad and laughing dog
  who wandered here a time.

II.

In evening, on the purple rise,
  with nighthawks wheeling free;
The orchard apples' rosy eyes
  peered down and laughed with me!

Gay robin, lend your minstrels here,
  while lark commands the flute,
For wind who sways the willow sprays
  hears music in the root!

Wild music fills this leafy hall
  when blackbirds bend the bough,
And every sparrow's bacchanal
  beats rhythm with the plow.

The ruby throat does winged ballet
  as it sips the chalice here.
The grumbling bee exacts his fee
  with scarce a sign of cheer!

Bright flowers raise their fluted cups
  to toast the sun in glee
While dandelions in yellow mirth
  race down the laughing lea!

The dragonfly who skims the pool,
  a sprite on fairy wing,

With jester's wand enchants the pond
    where nodding crickets sing.

In carousels of flaming blue
    the darning needles came.
Their torches brushed the goldenrod
    and set it all aflame!

The tadpoles, dressed like tailors,
    go threshing with their tails.
They gasp like foundered sailors
    who're sinking under sail.

They weave, they wind and wander
    in weird Saint Vitus dance—
All up-and-down in wonder
    as if they were entranced.

Indeed, they may be druids,
    or water nymphs, at least;
So sprightly, soft, and fluid,
    and pompous as a priest.

They're fat as golden Midas
    and silly as an oaf.
O, kindly Fates, retire us,
    like them, to lie and loaf!

III.

The sleeping rose awakens
    from Naiadean dreams
As volute petals, shaken,
    wake ripples on the stream.

The cottontail upraises,
    chagrined by hurrying dawn,
Where China lettuce lingers
    about the upland lawn.

The coyote and the bobcat
    lust for his furry throat;
The gimlet-eyed brown weasel
    prowls through the brushy moat.

How can the infant prosper
    through unprotected life?
The burrowing owls above him prowl
    with talons like a knife!

    The quail about him gather
        like sentinels on guard;
    The silhouetted squirrel
        stands listening in the yard.

    With every birdnote, every breath,
        the solitude they hear—
    The rustle of a feather,
        the footfall of a deer!

    O, who will guide and bade thee
        to fly, or guard thy fate;
    Will God, who fondly made thee
        in innocence *renait*?

    The startled dove will tell it
        with her vibrating wing.
    The routed quail distends it
        to every breathing thing!

    And who will spread the tiding
        like a crier in the street?
    The crested jay shouts warning
        and beats a quick retreat!

    He rants, he screams, he curses:
        It's very sad to tell.
    A monstrous hate he nurses
        and wishes no one well!

Yet, these are all your consort
    and wish you great good will
The meadowlark with sunny breast
    and liquid, bubbling trill.

The long-legged, long-eared rabbit,
    your cousin of the sage,
Will lure through endless habit
    the coyote in his rage.

They race along the rimrock
    through cedar in the glen,
And one must be the victor—
    but will they run again?

Down through the slashing bramble,
    the dry arroyo bed,
Through stone and croft they scramble
    as though all reason fled.

At last they reach the burrow
    beneath the lava stone.
A coyote gnashes gritted fangs
    and curses all alone.

IV.

How often we have hunted,
    this old brown dog and I,
Through grove and field enchanted,
    through grasses waving high;

Across the wide brook leaping,
    avaunt the lupined dale,
Around the sage-musked hummock,
    for rabbit, crow and quail;

Past froglet in the hollow
    with limpid, puffy eyes,
By coot who wends the mallow
    and crows with raucous cries.

The mallard bathes him daily
    along the rushy bank;
The meadowlarks call gaily
    beneath the willow's flank.

We waded wending rushes;
    we picked the currants—bright.
O, I had many comrades
    who shared in this delight!

The slingshot pebbles gathered,
    to bagging jeans dispersed,
A demon hunt we fostered
    as on the creek we burst.

The blackbird felt the onslaught,
    downed by our savage lust;
Our dogs would lead a rabbit chase
    in surging clouds of dust.

How soon we learned in childhood,
    who tried to mimic men,
How fate and fury, intertwined,
    destroy the rabbit den;

How falls the black crow, winging,
    hit by the raping rock
That stilled his raucous crying
    that death will ne're unlock.

We saw; we learned as children,
    how sad that this must be,
That men are cursed by th'burden
    of killing what is free!

Implanted in our being
    and coming from afar,
Lies cold instinct of killing—
    the harbinger of war.

We seem to reach in infancy
    to grasp Death's sinuous cord
As though it were a legacy
    to settle for the sword!

We saw our hounds, like vampires,
    thrill to the rabbit's blood;
It lit within us fires
    to kill the thing that moved!

And who shall change the fateful view
    that makes us tyrants all?
Is there but one—if any—who
    would lift us e'er we fall?

A voice comes back, "Come unto me,
    and I will give you rest."
O, noble Lord of Galilee
    upon the cross impressed!

V.

On the broad Snake's wide redress
    where the sphinx moth hovers,
Sipping nectar to excess
    in the lupined covers;

Sphinx Moth
Droz

There, lightfooted lads, we roamed
    through the gray sage brushes
Where the purling creek upfoamed,
    crystal in the rushes.

Where the green-robed perch leapt up
    and the plover tarried,
Where the greedy bee would sup,
    arrowheads were buried.

There we'd hunt while crows commuted,
    heard the blackbird's swelling song,
Sacked-and-stoned and pried-and-looted
    through all the summer long.

There we climbed the poplars sprightly,
    where the orchard pressed
As the cool breeze brushed them lightly
    with a fond caress.

There, the winding river brushes
    through the locks of graying sage,
And a waterfall down-rushes
    with pretended rage.

O, the wild, sweet sound that marches
    through the fairy-haunted glen
Where the vernal willow arches—
    never nearer God than then!

There the earth, and skies limned on it,
    seems a vap'rous sounding shell—
Like a singing, breathing sonnet
    threaded with supernal spell
        from the mount's enchanted well.

VI.

Yes, the wild, sweet sound that marched
    down that vernal willow-mead
Where the sago lily arched
    and the thirsty rushes feed,
Was as though our souls lay parched,
    and we feasted where they arched
      among the reed.

Where the breast of earth is beating
    in melody,
And the ranting creek makes fleeting
    minstrelsey,

Hear the lark's cajoling call
    through the marching poplar wall
When the violet tufted clouds
    lay like a sea.

Here, the wild kingfisher dove
    in the spume—
As the apple blossoms wove
    their perfume;

There, the oriole upflew
    from the grasses' glistening dew—
All the heaven that we knew
    was a-bloom!

Hear the breast of earth! It beats
    in harmony;
And the whispering wave entreats,
    "Lie here with me

On a haunted, murmuring isle
    where we'll linger for awhile,
Ere we race down golden tile
    to the sea!"

In a vast, wild conclavity of sound,
  while in golden chains of torpor
   we are bound,
Hear the ringing flower bells,
  like enchanted, vap'rous knells,
As their blessed music swells
  all around.

Would you linger where the glinting sunbeams fall
  over shadowed butte and piney canyon wall
Where the lava scarps lie meshed in purple thrall
  as the supple evening breeze
Sings a paean in the trees
  and the lonely owl laments with eerie call?

Hear the creek's low, lingering echoes as they pass
  on a poplar scented breeze through lazy grass,
And aspen groves that strum like tinkling glass—
  let nothing pass!
Where the blackbird hawks his wares in rushy mart
  art is nature—nature is her heart!

Wouldst not hear the chanting waters where they rise
  filled with multifidous-orbed dragonflies
Gathering all that tremblant splendor in their eyes?
  Summer sighs!
Listen softly. Hark, and listen where she lies—
  hear the soft notes—lifting—
   drifting—
    Alas! She dies!

"The Drop" by Dwight R. Droz

Songs of Shoshone River

Out of the riven cloud they burst,
Fresh from the virgin spheres,
Angel spirits in diamond-crypts,
Damped with the Pleiads' tears.
While thunder roars on mountain peaks,
And seraphs trail their wings,
The cold wind jars—assails the bars
Where an icy precipice clings.

So, out of the stormy night they come,
Fresh from the cloistered spheres
Bright drops dusted with diamond dew
Stained with Pleiads' tears.
They scatter o'er peaks of the Grand Tetons
On breasts of glistening snow
Like sparks that leap in a midnight fire
Or fade in the afterglow.

Their facets fill with a million lights!
They leap in crevassed-cloud:
A writhing spindrift 'round them trails
And curls in spiral shroud.
Supple to wend the roseate peaks
When sunset tints turn gold,
The northern lights dance fairy-rites
On crags so wild and cold.

A white goat strains on razor's-edge,
Balanced on a croft;
The eagle soars in broad ellipse
To keep track of his loft.
On summer nights when the owl's in flight,
As drops the silvery dew—
On such a night, the stars glow bright
And twinkle calm and blue.

Down fearsome rocks the night wind stalks
And roils the glistening snow;
It skims a ridge, an icy bridge,
And moans through wood below.
The summer's wren enjoys the glen
And nests in arbors cool;
The deer is fleet where life is sweet
Till Death invokes a rule.

Here lies the lair of a marmot pair,
Near pumas—lazed and dozing,
Where leaf-laced moons trace shadowed runes
While night winds lapse reposing.
Close by the weir, some geysers veer:
The creek's a silvery sliver;
And hawk moths[5] dart through laurel-thwarts
Along the Firehole river.

Out of the riven cloud it bursts,
Fresh from the whirling spheres,
An angel spirit felled from grace,
Dampened with Pleiads' tears—
Beautiful those trailing wings,
Brushed by purple stars,
Seared and singed, amaranthine wax,
Curling through heaven's bars.

---

[5] The hawk moth is cousin to the sphinx moth.

My waters rise in Teton's skies;
They leap the crevasse far
To span and foam a massif's dome
And roil the geyser bar:
As from the hushed, high peaks I rushed,
My ripples whirl and spill
To murmur on through graying dawn
True Molds Of Heaven's will.

Author's Note: The Snake was once called Shoshone River,
historians affirm. I'll never forget the boat ride above Shoshone
Falls on our graduation trip in 1931.

The Willow On The Hill
(Dedicated to Deanna's homecoming, November 27, 1966)

There's a sly old weeping willow
on a rillet by the hill,
Where a mill suns, and a rill runs
that is never ever still!

Down this hillet goes the rill,
ripples, chortling in its glee,
As a lad with pails to fill
laughs and whistles gay-a-lee!

On this treelet is a birdlet,
and his heart is full of note;
As the trills from his brown bill
tempts the mockingbird to rote.

Here, a maiden 'lies a dreaming'
of a knight who rounds the moat
Where-the-mill-is and-the-hill-is
as the bubbling cresses float.

There is a fox who softly stalks
by this rillet on the hill,
As he listens where it glistens
in a thicket, very still,
For a rabbit with gross habit
of far-roaming here at will!

O, it loves the tender grasses
where the calling whip-poor-will
Importunes with evening vespers
on this moonlit, haunted hill.

Girl and lad, gray fox and rabbit;
    softly singing whip-poor-will,
Shadowy knights and ghostly willows
    gathered at the purling rill!

Now! The quiet's ripped-asunder
    with abrupt and classic pace!
Fox and hare, exchanging glances,
    have encountered, face to face!

Then, a hound who smells the fox,
    comes, low-baying, around the bend;
As the fox pursues the rabbit
    in a race that soon must end!

Now, the boy comes wildly leaping
    down the rocky, rippling rill,
And he startled-up a partridge
    and the fluttering whip-poor-will.

All this consort comes a-tumbling
    to the bottom in a spill
Where a girl, in swift up-starting
    drops a slipper in the rill:

There she runs so nimbly after
    lad, fox, rabbit, shoe and rill
That she never—O, she never
    saw the knight so grand and still—

Or the dancing, milk white charger
    clothed in shadows—'neath the hill.

O, she brushed his golden tunic
    with her cheek and felt a thrill
Where the velvet shadows flickered:
    all the night was hushed and still.

How the knight was filled with longing,
    but his gray lips never spoke;
And a grim-and-leprous silence
    wrapped about him like a yoke!

Alas! She brushed by him, not knowing;
    through the abyss Death must face,
And she brushed his golden tunic,
    blindly flying in the chase
Of hounds, foxes, rabbits—birds,
    and "what nots" every place!

Yes, she touched his mail and tunic
    whose sad eye no tears could fill:
Where enchanted shadows linger
    neath the willow on the hill.

A Bullfrog Bulletin To Nature Lovers

We have a tree frog nesting on our back porch where the sun pours sumptuous beams all afternoon. He pants as he slants his torso like a pleasuring sun bather on the sands of Waikiki, careful not to get his feet wet, very wary of the sea.

I don't think tree frogs are for-real frogs though they have the hip and knee. There's more frisket in their brisket, though they never leave our lea. Like a sailor's son who isn't one (who skitters off to sea). Nature has some odd designers—a good example's thee. Our back porch knots with flower pots; and blossoms crowd its border. Folks who come, quite soon succumb to "pitter-pattic" order. Old watering pots, and scrubbing mops; a vase to tuck a bud in. A roll of string, in fact, anything folks cleaning a pocket lug in.

Pauline waylays some wild bouquets; picks zucchini prime for bashes, served to country boys with silly ploys and girls with blacked eyelashes. (We'll get back to the frog of this monologue before the syntax crashes.)

Our porch sign says: "The flower's are free: take what you want." Folks come to buy a book, have a chat—take a jaunt.

Main character of this treatise is a drifter impervious to rain; his moniker is Roger, who minds this brief refrain. With sticky knob feet he mans a seat on the rim of our windowpane. The fifth one up. He can really climb, he hops sometime, and he loves the porch light's glow! At eventide he stirs outside, come starlight, wind or foe. Roger carouses through darkening hours until the stars de-row!

He dozes in a black pot, most days—in a flower arrangement. There are several to choose from; Pauline

sees to that. He usually picks the corner pot, bidding strangers to kow tow. Roger is our Park Ranger and we know his croak by now. Roger reads the moods of our Scandia yen, in a secret code only tree frogs ken.

Pauline fills a teeny basin, his usual black pot, where a resident, unhesitant, bathes in a bottle cap. He's one and one-quarter inches long—a green-and-humpbacked-cog. A denizen, un-menacin' as an "Oregon waterdog."[6]

Our neighbor has another interloper, like Roger, residing on her porch. These intelligent amphibians are most adaptable. They truly enjoy the company of humans, luxuries of country dreamin' and electric lights. What an unusual sight! We walk by him hourly; he stares back with no chagrin. They have unique charm that warms the heart of a home. Mrs. Boehme, about two blocks hence, also had a frog move in. She found that a tiny birdhouse was just right for the frog to nap in. He too enjoys the privileges of country life. They share our goods, and roam our woods—don't pay a paltry cent—freeloaders, still, like "Barnacle Bill," unwilling to relent.

Protestors cry in years gone by, we drained the ponds and bogs. Bashing woods and in contretemps to environmental cogs. Now, the White House staff all fear this gaffe; voter's want to banish evil, don't treat the frogs and water dogs like you killed the droll, boll weevil!

Those newts and toads prove episodes of Nature's self reliance. We destroy, in disdain, the peak and plain—by meanly-mercurial giants! Bye! to frog-legs-Francine, in plates set serene—hot-sizzling in

---

[6] As a boy, we admired them at Vitae Springs, on the Willamette's bank. A crocodilic miniature with a froggish head and a rusty underbelly who loves fresh water springs.

roses and wine; chefs primped 'em in plastic; the meat was fantastic!   But, with wisdom, they attain a new shine.

You gay little buggers, we've become tree-frog-huggers. "Come on over to my house and flop. And once ya up and met us; be sure you don't forget us! You folks *are* hip—and tip-of-the-top!"

Patent Leather Slippers

Remember the days of 1910 and 1920. You don't? Be of strong heart. I'll refresh your mind. I was born the year the Titanic marched off her shipyard stocks and became a permanent submarine, for that's the year of my *néisance*. How nice it was, as a lad of eight, to climb in a buggy manned by Snukes, a mare—and Barney, not—on an open-carriage ride. Let's recreate the town of Rupert. On my feet are two sort-of "slippers," saucy, glossy and sedulously sedate:

They're of "Patent Leather"—
          a pompous black.
Too girlish (in a boy's mind);
          the memory flashes back.

I shuffle through the dust
          fussing all the while—
"Be good!" mama plead;
          I shook my head.
"Smile! cried mama.
          "SMILE!"

These were only for dress;
          and useless!
Down-track the horses splay.
          The bit rings snap,
Feet rat-a-tap,
          one lovely day in May!

We cross the bridge to Rupert; buggy wheels play a tune. We canter across Goat Island, a scene so

picayune. Meadowlarks are pleading, poplar catkins shower down, and a lateral stream enhances our dream as gay wheels spin around.

Who'd think a simple buggy ride can boost each sight and sound. The horses, nicker; our pace grows quicker. You wave at folk you know. A hamlet with a bandstand is the ideal place to go, less formal than a county fair or scrambling rodeo!

A Rupert Requiem

On the South stands parader's square, a Golden Rule Store is nestling there, selling clothing, yardage goods, shirts, skirts and comely hoods. There's a shoe bench at the front of the store where papa sat an hour or more. His crook pipe's fired, his mustache glows, and he's trading news with folks he knows.

A sales lad with soft city hands, and a most resplendent tie, beams at me; his face is lax as Madame Trousseau's show-room wax. I take a seat and sigh: I know what's comin'. By and by the salesman sights me. "Okay, son! What brand will you buy?"

"He needs dress shoes for church!" says dad in a brogue-ish voice, and I can tell I have no choice.

"A-ha!" says this tres-sharp chap, "patent leather oxfords are the best on tap."

And there they are on a mannequin—I look at the figure, with a grin. Dag-gone those patent-leather shoes, for city dandies and fashionados—not designed for mud-hole swales, hog-manure pitchers or lava trails. Such fancy duds and "tony knickers" weren't meant for bent potato pickers.

In those dumb clutts I feel a fool: we wore 'em Sundays as a rule. So, why did our women insist we try 'em? Why, in heaven, did papa buy em?

They didn't shield our feet from snakes;
had paper thin soles for sure;
Such culture's skewed for city dudes,
not farm boys, so impure,
I'm sure!

I didn't want 'em. Pa didn't either.
But mama rules.
My sisters said, "They're pretty in the city!"
Pop drained his purse—and, what is worse,
I got no trace of pity.
Kids get stuck in nitty-gritty
by an "Adult-Rules Committee."

We're at Rupert park. Day is Fourth of July. Wonders continue as we walk by. Most stores are closed, and we romp in good weather past stands lined with bunting, hammered together. Girls in straw hats with flimsy gowns are like a show at Upland Downs. A Chamber of Commerce booth boasts a bungling clown. Lovers spark in the park as fireworks bound. Rockets loft, sparklers flare; what beastly racket fills the air! Cannon crackers roar and spit. Not long before you tire of it! Kilgore cap-guns we bought, are cheap-o-made; they sputter and balk. We made big faces when they'd *sput*; paraders menace one another.

A late-schoolmate sneaks up on me, that neighbor kid who stutters. He waves two pop guns in the sun. "Now-w-w! Fi-i-ite fer ya' li-i-fe!" he mutters as loud as he can.

I rouse at the insult; our lips are tight. Were "duking-it out" with popguns, right? My left hand clutches the hem of my pants cut short-at-knee. Those darn brigands, with elastic bands, do really booger me. I shoot! They slup! I pull 'em up, though golf nuts let 'em flop.

Hike 'em with your left; aim the gat with your right. What a miserable way on such a fine day to frame a duel, right?

During this chat, I wear a sheep-wool cap Mom knitted two years ago—a bit-o-monument of splat! She deemed it "cool" for Sunday school, from December through July. So, on my dome parks this ham bone, stuck with it till I die!

What a canard—I'm battling hard; I feel my psyche lapse. My enemy is shooting hot—am I outa' Kilgore caps! Perhaps? Any fool can "wiss" who won in this "Last Chance Saloon" foray. It was here, I learned, a mantra churned, I remember to this day: "Never fight duels with duds that slop, in a knit-wool cap with a pesky flop."

Everyone snickers. My neighbors yell: *"Pull up your knickers!"* I remember it all well.

Those Dowdy Shoes

My patent shoes flapped as I walked;
     the soles were bland-and-bleak.
Sunday-morn-to-supper-time,
     we donned those piddley-tweaks.
I felt sad as an undertaker
     on pound-the-pulpit weeks!

Now, all my family thought it grand
     that I wore the little "nippers";
Other boys laughed at my silly shoes
     before the day of zippers.

There was a rage called the "cootie-cage,"
     buns of hair, twenties styles decreed.
Combed and domed in a puffy-pile,
     along with baubles and beads.

So here's a lad—a simple tad—
    in a land of ribbons and bows:
Gals with hair-to-floor, customs galore,
    small boys in knickers and hose:
So childhood goes! Led by the nose!
    With few "yo ho's!"

As I said, we wore the "pretty shoes" on Sunday. Mondays, we went barefoot in revenge. For that act we paid an uncomfortable price. We got stickers in our soles and toes. Who gets the blame for this plaint we frame? Not some *Aleut* with a "humongous" snoot—not the Vikings or Prussians; so whiskered galoots in big black boots gain roguish repercussions. Claim they deserve a curse that's bad or worse—so evil the Devil blushes!

I'm talking about thistles, here. There are devil clubs in Olympian-scrubs. There's cactus in the pines. And in the South, don't shut my mouth, are horrible kudzu vines—as thick as cactus spines. There are beastly tones of bristle cones. Saguaros prick your shin, and cholla may annoy-ya worse than the fangs on Rin Tin Tin. There is a plant, cruel as an ant, a miserable beast of pray. A proven cheater, like the dust bowl skeeter, plaguing every right of way. It's an import of the cruelest sort, in many ways prior to days of nucleonic missiles.

Weeds sneaked to America on a ship—those damnable Russian thistles!

We pick them out of our hides at night or during daylight hours. You find their ranks on old ditch banks, or circling ivory towers. On a canal trip where you "skinny dip," they puncture your behinder. It chokes fields of grain, causes bare-hand pain, shocking sheaves behind the binder. What a grinder!

Marvelous little cutters; with scads of spiny teeth. It loves to meld with a human shell on meadow, moor and heath. It travels with the sagebrush—lines every country road. It stumbles over every spot where yellow mustard strode.

Your feet grow tougher by the time it's fall. But my hide never toughens up at all. I limp all day, hoping night will call. I'm sad my barefoot days are through; good-bye old comrades; I sure miss you!

We had few toys in early years, made playthings out of broken gears. A rusty band of an old wheel hub made rolling hoops with a bit of scrub. Use a "tickling-stick" to keep it spinning. Old buggy wheels are well worth winning. Down lane, you head for lights of home, trailing through sage—a way to roam! You loved a dip in the cold canal. (I miss you, Oran. You were a pal!)

Along the road, old tires are sunning. Gather up the castaways, and soon the place is humming. That Huntsman boy loved to tinker up some scheme. He found a beat up coaster; dragged wheels out of a stream. His papa, Hiram, helped him build one "bob-wire" limousine! Takes no oil or gas to run first class—no payments so obscene. It was the best "old coaster"—and here I toast'er!—that ever hit the street. We drove that bugger every where, sittin' on our derriere, powered by our feet!

Our lips made sounds of action.
"Rev-v-v the motor! Brr-r-r-uff!"
There wasn't a lot of yellin';
there was just enough!
"BANG! BANG!" our voices rang.
"All aboard. O, Feel it lug!
Pause for passengers!" Oran sang,
conductor of the 'bug'.

Sometimes it was an Oldsmobile—
more oft', a railroad train;
I only wish that I could ride
that haywire-squire again!

"Olay!" Those were good days,
with tassels on the corn.
At morn, a blushing sun is born.
Meadow grass rolls in the jaunty breeze
paging barefoot boys
with 'holey' knees.

Sparrows quarrel in the poplar trees;
a lark is "bustin'-rib" with song.
We roam and dream—all summer long—
a life of promises filled with joy,
when I was a barefoot boy.

Rabbits sprang; hawks wheeled overhead—
mumble a prayer; you're off to bed!

Children wild as antelopes try to out lope ya;
even so it wasn't Utopia. There were trials for all, I
guess. Jackrabbit warble flies caused great distress.
Meat was often scarce in camp at the century's end,
so…"into Gypsy's pots, them rabbits got; it sure was
poor-man's-chicken."

Cottontails were choice 'assize'; popping out of
lava-dives, aimed for batholiths on yonder rise—a
place they're safe from prying eyes.

Settlers at Cotterel had to utilize any scraps
available on the homestead, like dandelion salad, dug
for Easter snacks, drowned with vinegar, egg-garlands
and mashed potatoes. How good this all tasted! Red
pigweed and lamb's quarter greens were delightful.
Grasshopper fat chickens, or plump geese, lined the
platter, and Jersey butter glowed on every plate.

Outside this banquet table, wheat plantings soon failed. The sky was gleaned of clouds; grim winds pried new seed out of the earth before it could sprout! And Cotterel was no more!

All those men who cleared the land fled the desert in the end. Only rabbits, hawks, ground squirrels, and a few other denizens remained. I nearly forget the hard times as years trek onward. Funny, I don't think I'll ever forget getting dressed for Sunday services—'bedecked-and-be-danged' in patent leather slippers with knickers nagging my knees. No more of that foo-fra, pa! Don't make me wear 'em— please!

The Boomer

When men are young all facts are clear.
We've little sense and scanty fear.
The world's a bubble and you know it;
You persevere—and then you blow it!

I once was a poor and lonely student.
Very trustful—oft imprudent—
This is a true tale of one erstwhile roomer:
A unique chap! Call him "The Boomer!"
A Charles Dickens sort of sprite.
I've a tale to tell, painful to write;
I wonder where he rests tonight.

"Hey, Stude," says Darren's girl at school
(where Sphinx Business College sets the rule.) "This
chap ya often harbor where the boy friend[7] parks, is
sure a 'problem-nut', and a cool pool-shark!"

She says, "Tell me! What's he up to when the
alleys all go dark?"

"You make him so ominous!" I warn with a
grin. "Is every foamin' roamer a barrel of sin? This
chap sets pins in Bowling Alley 'Y'. So! He coppers
my shirts and dons Darren's tie! He's merely street-
wise, so I surmise; we'll cure him, bye and bye!"

                        ⌛

---

[7] The name is fictitious but the story is true. He died years ago. The
finest roommate I ever knew.

Pause A Moment!

This is the message of my tome
a reason for this tale:
"If you try to train a balky mule,
let 'donkey ways' prevail!"
I once was quite-foolish,
though thought I was wise.
I had to improve something;
just one of my tries—
But all that I gained
was *wrinkle-wracked-eyes*!

I face Darren's girl with a friendly grin. "He talks big talk—he's had it tough! He'll find new spaces soon enough. It's true he's a loner; misfits love talk. He's an orphaned kid, on a skid, whose racing with the clock and brags of BIG investments and raunchy poppy-cock.

"It's just a 'put-on'; he hasn't a dime. Just wait a few weeks; the change will take time!"

"Why do you tolerate him?" asks my roommate friend.

"I figure he needs help," I say. "He may improve in the end!"

"D" gave me "the-look" and heaved a big sigh. (Now, as I post, they're both a ghost—and nearly that am I!)

⌛

Of all the words I ever penned, 'twixt-my-birthday and the tomb, this Ebenezer's one gaffe of a rather fulgent bloom! Perhaps the silliest-ever-kenned with a-poc-a-lyp-tic[8] gloom!

Darren is a friendly chap, a happy type of chum who chips in a few shekels when our rent collectors come. His girlfriend oft complained that our pinsetter[9] distraught her. Finance-wise she can't surmise that I'm belly-deep in water! Very little Darren taught'er!

Though the Boomer's a third-pick-roomer, he has Bowery-Skills indeed and knows ways to stretch a dollar, a big help in times of need!

Socially lagging in our setup; he becomes a piggy bank, this buccaneerish-pirate so adept at "walk-the-plank." He brings candy bars and honey—here's another trib to rank: his speech is *rather* funny! That 'poolhall-alley' cat! If you're growing short of patience, win a feeble grin from that!

I hand him one buck. "Pray, fetch me milk, along with buns and beans." He dons his mitts—picks up the list—shoves the dollar in his jeans.

That evening he works a few blocks down, returns with *booty*—best in town, a quart of cream!—(That chap could scheme!) plus two loaves "plump-and-brown." Two cans of beans, hid in his jeans, and proudly clumps 'em down.

⏳

---

[8] Apocalyptic in an old-and-weathered dictionary reads: 1. Containing or pertaining to revelation; disclosing. 2. Pertaining to the Apocalypse. [Also] *Apocalyptic number;* the number 666, spoken of in Rev. xiii.18.
[9] Bowling alley of the thirties were a hard-knock place! Pins were 'manually' SET. Those 'pin boys' perched on a shelf directly over the 'tumbling target'—a dangerous place to work!

Did he snatch the milk from a neighbor stoop,
    as quick as Alley Oop,[10]
Where he wangled dough for this a can of soup,
    I guess I'll never know;
Marched in with a grin, as brash as *sin*,
    so full of zip-and-go.
Playing tricky-feats, even on dead-beats,
    that clever Gypsies trow!

We're in a bad depression—
    money's tight as any bolt.
Will Roosevelt help-belt the wolf,
    as, hopelessly, we "moult?"
The Oakies came to join the game;
    or to California hied....
Like passing ships *cross-in-the-night*,
    awander with the tide!
Ragged tots, on every spot—
    shabbily-dressed and woebegone!
Past grave-side-plots and weedy lots,
    the drifters muddle on!

⏳

Now, back to our story; hop on—join the ride!
Student's at the Business College, doing odd-jobs on the
side. He tries to counsel Boomer; thinking "B" will
soon *fly right*—hoping that, with *patient guidance*,
"Boom" will finally see the light!

Stude and Darren, really revvin',
    loudly snore from ten-to-seven.
Boomer cat-naps late each morn
    with no intention to reform.

---

[10] A notorious cut-up of early Funny Paper comedians. Perhaps
that was before your time.

He promises profs to pay the bill;
    perhaps, in 3002, he will!

When someone's striving vainly—
    and you spot the schedule's *tight*,
Some do-gooder's bound to *tap it*,
    worrying the plan's too trite.
Then two counselors hop in
    and devour 'im with delight!
The Student's bound to worry
    as the Boomer's lot grew worse.
Truth is: "Oft our early years
    host enigmas of reverse!"
I do believe "this writer" was
    the one friend Boomer got.
My guess: today, his bones parlay
    in a weedy, lonely plot!

⧗

Final Memories

"Last week we needed a quart of milk. Fifty cents was all I had; Boomer came back in an hour— with a quart of cream "Bedad!" This made a dandy breakfast with corn-flakes *a la bowl*. You couldn't fail to see the Boomer really knew his "hobo role."
    Oftentimes the Student tensed, sensing mayhem in the ranks: "If you ever cheat me Boomer; if you tap my piggy-banks, that will dent my sense of humor; don't pull any fancy pranks!"
    Sometimes he, the Student, would say, in view of how little money was spent, "I am a little puzzled how you purchased all this cream!"
    Outside, the wolf comports a séance; depression lingers 'round our shack; to insults he's pro-impervious

when night-wolves prowl in pack. That obstreperous, sappy schemer touts his Bowery-skills we lack! He'd find ways to stretch a dollar—and then get a halver back!

Boomer flashed those big, white teeth—this Cajun, full of tricks. Well, his pop was French-Canadian—he's a *very devious* mix!

"Well," he said, "I was just lucky; there's a Grocer's Special Sale. There wuz lettuce in the dumpster better than they served in jail! Just clip a leaf, trim a sheaf. Presto! *Salado-Au-Pail!*"

I still see him, grinning widely, as we share a Soup-Cocktail! But my suspicion is:

> Was it pilfered from a doorstep
> while the resident was gone?
> Due to this, we'd fuller bellies—
> the Depression just rolled on!

> Life was bleak in Boise City
> so the Student let him stay!
> AND…he never stole *one* dime from me
> unto his dying day!"

⌛

Epilogue

The Boomer finally left Boise to find new pastures. He and the student went their separate ways. It's evident he had no intention of performing honest toil. Does he moulder in this nation, or claim Canadian soil?

End of an era. Close the tale. Somewhere, smack in the "out-back," is he possibly in jail?

He once delivered flowers;
    most honest job in sight.
He could be kind and thoughtful,
    but things never came out right.
At heart he was a gypsy
    and finally found the light.
Simple workdays were bland;
    the format too stale.
Sharp tricks were more exciting—
    who cares a nit 'bout jail?

Cajun revelers enjoy every tide!
Some rascals long for risks untried—
And gypsy roads do beckon wide.

The Boomer chose the "conner-ken,"
Following paths of *wasted-men*!
He'll never cross our sill again!

The End

Ragweed
(or "Two Tavern Poets")

When I arrived in Seattle on June 16, 1942, the city was booming with war workers, sailors, and folks from Maine or Minnesota who left the family farm, or the city, to work in war plants because Roosevelt said the war effort needed us—and it was true.

Tires were rationed, travel restricted, and "Share-the-Ride" we did with pride. I climbed on the Kalakala, jouncing and bouncing though tide rips. As I ogled the gulls, peering through a multitude of oval windows, a merchant ship hove into view. The stacks were spouting smoke; the flag had an Oriental name; I was enthralled.

My life in Bremerton held one surprise after another for a landlubber from Boise who had never known Puget Sound's hills and valleys could be so green. In the weeks that followed I rambled around the town Mr. Bremer practically owned "lock-stock-and-barrel"; searching for a good place to eat I came upon a *Bar-&-Grill* near the waterfront. I was soupin'-up hungry and lonely, and I overheard two spry young chaps in the booth next to me plotting-and-planning to telegram a friend somewhere east of the mountains. Was it Yakima, or Twin?

Point was, the party they were telegraphing was mobile, not bound to the Navy Yard as I was. And these two lads seemed blithe and happy. Was the recipient of the message a lady? I'll never know; but out here where the cedars grow and Olympian Towers rise and glow, I know these fellows had the stuff to make that visit grand enough. They knew how to entertain.

Thinking of entertaining, my mind drifts back to Ivar Haglund of Puget Sound fame, one of the finest

singers around, with easy guitars and western slang he wrote these lines and happily sang: "I've traveled all over this country, and never in life have I found, a place that's more peaceful and quiet, than livin' on Ol' Puget Sound. No longer the slave of ambition, I scoff at pretenses and shams, to sing of my happy condition, surrounded by acres of clams!"[11] Well, Ivar, that's how I heard it on the air; hope you'll let me quote you; we shared the same hours—but you're no longer with us.

His irrepressible *joie de vivre* enthusiasm, coupled with his *kabiz* of earning bucks with salmon bakes or "gooey-ducks" melds here with Stan Boreson and his lazy-eyed hound who acted "the rogue" as Stan *accordioned* in Swedish brogue. Why am I off on such a tack? To highlight skills most diners lack; it is a pleasure to bring 'em back!

Here's how the discussion continues in the booth next to mine: "How will we word the telegram?" asked a lad with a curly mop, hefting a beer mug combed with foam on top. "Oh E-Z!" chimed his pal. "How about?"

> "We are here—an' you are there—
>   but, ragweed pollen's in the air!"
> The other agreed and added,
>   "So, why not come, relaxed and limber
> To Puget Sound's resounding timber."

I was listening, surprise inflating. Who says poetry is *decidating*? These two have the class of a college in Mass—it ends with *chusetts* don't give me no sass. The sharpest of those beer-muggin' scribes speaks as follows; and here's how he vibes:

---

[11] Actually, the first stanza of the famous verse goes like this: "No longer the slave of ambition / I laugh at the world and its shams / As I think of my happy condition / Surrounded by acres of clams."

"Why not celebrate Independence Day
    in some special sort of way?
So fly out where the blue tides roll
    and latch some sunshine in your soul!
"So come on down, relaxed and limber,
    to Puget Sound's resounding timber!"

I dubbed in a two-line finale;
    I think it fits here well, by golly!
A sane and sonorous encore:
    "Bon exitas and au revoir."

Metes And Bounds

A humorous title company executive in Washington state, Babe Campbell, often joked about a deed, framed and hung on an abstract office wall: "Starting from an ax driven in a woodpile...." One does tend to ponder how long axes remain un-budged in busy frontier wood piles.

Mr. Campbell, a close friend, finally passed away a few years back, but his illuminating lessons in title posting remain in mind as I write.

Early-day deeds were classics of adaptation, risk, hurry and creativity. Land was cheap, boundaries were vague, saplings and stumps, rocks and dumps, all play a role in this frontier sketch.

When my brother, Luke, was County Assessor, he came across one unusual boundary description that read: "Starting from a knothole in the Albion Jail...." That was the point of beginning (P.O.B.). In those times, country folks often used a sapling or a rock in early deed boundary descriptions.

That P.O.B. in Albion Jail survived remarkably well, for many years. Truth is, this jail, first ever built, I surmise, held one especially notorious prisoner, Diamondfield Jack, arrested on suspicion of killing a sheepherder in cold blood. A range war was imminent.

Albion was considered cattle country. Sheep were not liked because they trimmed the grass too close. That shooting episode rocked the entire state, and much of the West.

A group had gathered. The gallows stood ready, a "Perils-Of-Pauline"-like episode; but, before the noose snapped, a lathered horse came on a wobbly gallop over the Albion rim with a weary rider named Sears—and a governor's pardon.

That ancient jail, partially from this notorious incident, became a national shrine—of sorts. Somewhere I read it was eventually moved to Oakley. Albion Normal School had shut down and that fine old town was "thin of feather" as a robin's tot in May. I don't know whether the move is true, but I certainly remember the jail.

Those old timers were "down-home" folks. That primitive way of writing deeds supports this idea.

I spent eighteen months as poster and chainer in Washington Title Company in Bremerton. The job requires careful-cursives penmanship, patience and map work. Here, I learned property descriptions are of two types: (1) Metes and Bounds; (2) Lot and Block.

Date is September 16, 1981. Let me now introduce a hopeful kid, who thought he was a writer. That "lad in the frame" got quite a nudge from one well-known escrow officer and abstractor who remains nameless. He is green as pumpkin vine curls, tracking Cotterel history that September morn. That lad heads for Cassia County Court House.

Time's 1:30 PM. Pleasant personnel lead him to archives; they wake the slumbering tract books, open sleepy pages, and settlers long forgotten rose from the yellowing sheets, yawned and stepped out on unsteady feet. Yes, we know that's whimsical nonsense—but this was a plat—brimful of stories to glean. Here were the names of Hausens, Kulms, Kessingers and Schrenks. He'd never seen the Kulms; the rest he had met, years after Cotterel licked its wounds and stole away. I repeat this mild vignette explains, in a simple way, why country lads find no merciful havens in large city mavens, or habitations.

It's a mild roast of an escrower's ghost. Please join us. The lad and this old octogenarian, cogitating and remembering. That feral, roaming tomcat, with pen

and tablet in hand, went to Burley full of anticipatory
vibrations, remembering the days of his earlier youth:

To search the shards of boulevards
        and peer in old archives.
The court house folks, those friendly blokes,
        helped recreate past lives.
I copied names of trails they trod,[12]
        with maps in store,
Bang the courthouse door
        and right up Overland plods.

I usually lunch that time of day,
        and head my bones to Griz-cafe.
One hour's spent—now I'm escrow bent
        at an abstractor's digs. I pipe, "Hello!
I'm D. R. Droz, youngest in rank;
        my family's last ancestor.
My brother, employed at a mortgage bank,
        became the County Assessor.

"My father farmed sections 23 and 26;
        our efforts came to nix—
An unholy scrabble of ruined ways,
        back in the Sam Cotterel days.
One of many settlers who lost a tract;
        $37.88 in taxes is what we lacked."

That abstractor knew my family;
        he knew my brother well.
He'd heard that Cotterel tale before;
        old history; nothing more.
Point on his mind is: "Get your fee;
        old news clips are gypping me!"

---

[12] California Trail, The Indian Trace, Oregon Trail and more were
portrayed on the county maps.

He calls a lady, perched on a stool,
    says, "Fetch a tract book from the pool."
Those were copies of my courthouse rotes,
    when all I sought was backup notes.
The old bugger sits, the book in-his-mitts:
    "I want 75 bucks for abstract kits."
It's clear he thrives on nitzy bits,
    and loves the *dough-re-me* he gits!

"I'm writing a book on Cotterel," I admit, mildly shook:
    "I don't need abstracts—just want a quick look.
I came to ask historic facts
    about Sam, his plat, and map of tracts."
He's disappointed but shouldn't *flup*;
    says he, "You'll have to rent this book."
He lifts the bugger up—
    like the plates of Moses.
"Here's what I have; all of the facts;
    scan 20 minutes—20 bucks, no tax!"

On spur of the moment, I paid for a look;
    it didn't seem worth the time it took.
A scrivener of Cassian glades,
    and Chamber of Commerce escapades.

Seated in that weathered chair,
    rakes me with a doleful stare;
Muses, this nutty and boorish prank
    badly interrupts my trip to the bank.
These Decloans are "callous-dumbs";
    and still, this silly settler comes.
A stupid boob who claims he writes;
    did he guzzle too many Miller-Lights?
Says he's O. Henry, born again;
    shoo-away! Clear out and get lost!
        Amen!

A final question ends this tale:
    "Is that knothole still sound
        on the wall of Albion jail?"

Vitae Springs Trilogy

"Fall on Green Mountain" by Dwight R. Droz

Big Times On "F" Street

Independence, Oregon.

What a lovely old town it was.

Touring cars sported isinglass curtains and light blue fenders crying to be despoiled by mud. You could lounge outside, riding on the fenders, cruising dirt roads in the outback. It would take a designer's promotion man to describe that wonderful Chevrolet we owned when I finished seventh grade. Wilderness was never far away. You couldn't ignore a road because of ruts and washboard ripples. Dad huffed hard on his polished brown pipe, roaring through mud-or-scud— whoopee!

"Watch me put 'er through, son," Dad admonished, when we hit the second bad stretch. He had great faith in Chevies from Detroit. Things were going quite well about that time. Good thing Dad couldn't see far beyond that proud old Swiss-Roman nose. I believe our clan in Switzerland must have had that distinctive mark across a wide swath of mountains and peaks. The Humbert-Droz nose, I call it. All the children had signs of it, but I liked pop's the best. His clipped mustache with a trace of a sag at the corner fit that aristocratic "schnoz" to a slick-tee.

"The Humbert-Droz Nose"

This was the early part of the twenties. We were beginning to get our feet set on that spunky Idaho loam that grew beautiful potatoes, swollen beets and aromatic Lucerne hay. Our horses were

fat; our jerseys had seven percent butterfat when the twenties were picking up steam.

The girls were about to launch into hobble skirts and bucket hats—and weren't they somethin'! I was a kid, and a country kid at that, but I still remember there was a jaunty feeling in the air, when you fitted the radiator cap figurine with a holder and had five small flags billowing on the Fourth of July. You had a fulltime job on Sunday just hitching up those long black stockings small boys wore, trying to make those silly knee-knickers stay above your knees. I never want to go through that again!

Times were moving fast. My brothers and sisters grew up like corn stalks, and I was caught in the time warp. Mother wanted my sisters to go to Normal School. They had attended Albion, but for reasons I fail to remember mother decided to move one of my brothers and both my sisters to Oregon for a year. Sisters May and Dora planned to complete their teacher's training there. So, out of sunny Idaho we spun in a new-and-blue Chevrolet fast on our way to the vapory autumn skies of Oregon woodlands. Queen Anne's Lace greeted us on dusty treks as we searched for a place to stay the year. We tried to locate a house in the country, but none were suitable or reasonably priced; but then we rented a little place on "F' Street, in Independence, Oregon, a short distance from Monmouth Normal School. We were thrilled!

Mom, Luke, May, Dora, and I settled in for an Oregon experience. This was the year radio came to the fore, and we felt we were in the beginning of a new and grand millennium. My father, along with Roy, my oldest brother, remained in Idaho to run the farm.

The city of Independence made Declo unreal. Would you believe it—all of Oregon's important streets were of tar. We, had always been used to dust, lava

rock and random swatches of gravel on our by-ways, with washboards and chuck holes galore. But tar! What luxury!

Yes, Oregon was a surprise to every one. Independence had rural flavor as well. Along the side walks, the sloughs were replete with hazel bushes and hosts of huge oaks draped with moss and mistletoe. What wonderful vistas for sagebrush stoics. The miracle was these plants survived without irrigation. This was unbelievable to a desert lad raised on *dry farms*. Houses seemed so close together in the city. All was new.

Heading a few blocks north and east brought a stroller to the heart of a mini city glowing on a scenic plateau just above the calm-faced Willamette River, with, of all things, a cable ferry. I was delighted and so was my family.

Electric ferry crossing Willamette River, Independence, Oregon, circa 1939 (Ben Maxwell, Photo:7328).

Large oaks lounged provokingly, inviting us to romp. How lush and lusty were the ripe blackberries. A musty odor livened the Oregon woodlands. Hazel bushes and shaggy ferns lay far removed from the sagebrush plains of Cassia County, Idaho.

To a boy of thirteen, everything new was glamorous. Adventure awaited you every morning. Sprinkled with oaks and crowned with mistletoe, lush meadows wakened even a mummy. As I said, the town was north and east of our new home on "F" Street. There were so few businesses, you could saunter by the whole shebang in a short walk. Most important of all, the Isis Theater glowed over the main street.

The Isis Theater closed in 1958, but in the mid-1920s it was the Eight Wonder of the World! (Ben Maxwell, Photo:6266)

Radio was just coming in. The Isis boasted a large cabinet radio that blared whatever was going on in Portland at the time. The Isis manager turned it on during intermissions so you could hear this magic machine—and it still is magic, play and talk, wonder of wonders!

Life seemed more staid, safe and settled than we had ever known it in Declo. No toughs threatened to kick or rob us—not a one! Rather, everyone wore ties and dress clothes, not overalls. I must say, it was like entering a monastery after leaving a battleground. Hardly any Mormons lived here, either. I must apologize to my Mormon friends, but most kids in Declo were clannish. Good Mormons weren't so unfriendly, but, most of the time, we were outsiders; in Independence, Oregon, we weren't second class citizens.

After the ashes of 75 years have cooled, it's hard to recapture those childhood years. Here are some of the best examples this child remembers.

The Junkman

There was a junkman in old Independence.

Every small town has them.

As the story goes, three boys hiked along the Willamette one afternoon. Among lofty oaks with moss and mistletoe gleaming lay an abandoned gravel bunker. Most of it's massive corpse had disappeared, stripped by vandals and floods, and only a few planks and little hardware remained.

The boys pulled a fine red wagon with a hardwood cargo box, blue-striped for beauty's sake. They dragged this fancy bit right to the bunker and gazed in awe at the remains. There among towering oaks and musty odors reposed a cache of copper wires. We were overjoyed!

I cannot remember what copper was worth in the mid-1920s, *inflation* had not been coined yet. There was over a quarter's worth for each of us, that much we knew. So eager hearts loaded the cables onto that nifty wagon, and we hustled to town, pulling by turns. It was a good mile.

The junkman viewed us with kind pity; we were sweaty and scuffed, but everyone wore a smile. He didn't ask where we found it; insulation came and went along that roll. The junker weighed it.

I liked to believe he relived his childhood for a moment, thinking what he'd buy, thinking he was one of us three small lads with a quarter each to "blow." I think he paid us every cent the wire was worth because of it—bless him!

How few adults, then or today, really strive to give a child his due—if no one watches. All my grown life I ponder how hard and unjust life is to small children. People look down and rule you. If only they would come down to our level more often.

The Crippled Man

There was an old man right across the street from our house on "F" Street. He had a florid face, walked with a cane and swung down the track on a hand-whittled peg leg. He lived in a one-room depression-shack. He had whittled his false leg from rough boards and fashioned the fork as well; this clumsy device used leather harness straps and buckles to bind it to his thigh. He never painted it; in the middle of its top was a saucer-shaped pit in

Old man
Hobbling
in the Garden!

Droz

which he placed rags or toweling, whatever came to hand. This self-made wonder had little compassion for the stump—but he got by.

Never having married, that old man was lonely.

He encouraged me to visit. I'll never forget that one time I went over to his little gray home. A coal-oil heater warmed the room that day, but I saw the walls were unfinished and felt a cold draft. Naked two-by-fours held up the walls. One layer of building paper does little to hold out the wintry blasts.

Two-by-fours are spectral at best; he nailed in a few shelves for knick-knacks, clocks, razors and mugs. Inventive souls find many nooks for foo-fras on musty cabin walls.

> Don't look for Beauty Here;
>   all you get is the drab-and-drear!
> You keep the hammer on a spike
>   and use as many boardy-bits,
> There's space enough to strike.
>
> Hammer bent nails straight again,
>   tack tin cans over knots.
> On barren walls you want some dreams,
>   along with gadget needs
> Like violets mid the weeds;
>   a pic of some departed love—
> Until Death intercedes!

And that is how a cabin grows; that's how our needs are planned as wiser, lonelier you grow; but few folks understand.

His digs barely concealed pits and scratches of poverty he wouldn't admit. He was proud. The blue overalls were faded, too often scrubbed. His handlebar mustache had a scraggly mien. He was well-shaven at the cheek. He was old. His eye was meek. He was a battered eagle who could no longer soar. Death was ever watchful, in wait beside his door.

> The wolf went by, his nose held high;
>   he'd known him heretofore.

He did not lounge around the yard;
　　his attitude was plain.
By Poverty that door was barred;
　　a smitch of some departed love—
　　　　there's nothing here to gain.

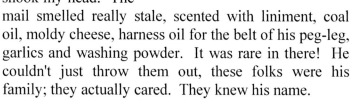

Inside the cabin was the overpowering scent of kerosene mingled with the strong emanations of Absorbine liniment—for old bones. After half an hour, senses collapse. Ol' Pegleg was lonely; that much was clear. His cabin was crammed with junk mail: insurance offers, vacuum sales, you name it!

"Would ya like some of these?" he asked, holding out the mail.

"Well, no!" I shook my head. The mail smelled really stale, scented with liniment, coal oil, moldy cheese, harness oil for the belt of his peg-leg, garlics and washing powder. It was rare in there! He couldn't just throw them out, these folks were his family; they actually cared. They knew his name.

I prepared to leave, nothing could exist in this atmosphere, outside of a rugged old man blessed with the warmth of a kerosene heater and the relieving powers of liniment—bugger the smell! This is the lot of an aging pauper who gardens a bit in spite of sprains and pains, harassed by creaking leather bands and the uncomfortable pegleg. If you're eminently lonely, it's nice to get mail right at your very door from folks in high buildings with marble columns, the seats of grace.

"You can have all of these, too," he said. Guess what he mainly ate: Quaker Oats. There were dozens

of those round containers piled everywhere. "I seldom cook," he added. "I soak th'oats in water, simmer 'em now and then, they're pretty good raw. It's bad to cook stuff too much!"

I teared as he spoke. His eyes held a serious gleam. I swallowed hard, thinking of eating raw oatmeal days on end. I felt compassion for this old mongrel. We talked of ships and sealing wax and other things. Finally, it was time to come up for air. Pegleg followed me out, surveying the ground with great care before putting weight on his peg.

"Gotta be careful," he advised. "If I step in mole burrows, it'll tip me over!"

I never laughed. Wooden legs are not funny, of course. Poverty took all the fun out of us there.

Hops Fields

Hops grew on long trellises on the flats by the Willamette—fields of hops have a marvelous smell. It attracts, when minimal, and overpowers your nose, when concentrated.

"there wuz miles of hops on wires"

Regular hop pickers wrapped their fingers with friction tape to protect them from the abrasion of vines and leaves as they stripped the blossoms into waist high baskets.

Two capacious baskets packed tightly weighed around 40 pounds. It took quite a while for a novice to fill two baskets—no doubt experienced people were able to excel at this. It was no bonanza, needless to say.

Hops on wires ~ year 1926

"I'd much rather pick big Idaho potatoes," my brother Luke opined. "I can get my mitts on them a lot better."

I grinned and ruefully eyed stained fingers and blisters from a few hours grind.

"Me too!" I said.

That was the last time we entered a hop field in Oregon.

Hop Wagon

Hop pickers camp, Eola, near the fields around
Independence, circa 1939 (Ben Maxwell, Photo:6259).

People in Independence often talked about the goings-on in camps at hop picking time. There were knifings, family feuds, quarrels, murders, lesser orgies and general mayhem. Remember, these were prohibition days. The roaring twenties were howling full blast. Workers often cured their woes with alcohol on a weekend fling. Liquor bottles were oval shaped to fit your pocket and avoid detection by Revenuers.

Small Hop Barn

Empties lay strewn about in alleys and barrow pits. Often the drinker, by habit, replaced the cork even after a pint was emptied. We opened them to sniff the raw-sweet odor. It tickled the nose and smelled like nothing else. There was always some residue.

It was not unusual to find partially filled bottles stashed in odd places, and sometimes full pints were cached in outbuildings. There was always the need to outsmart the sheriff. The owner of a flagon could return after chores, or after supper to take a short-snort before bedtime. Perhaps he was married, and his wife frowned on drink.

Independence, like other towns had unique die-hards who enjoyed the distinction of being known as a tough fellow. Bootlegging was both profitable and hazardous. Booze was linked closely to crime, houses of prostitution and gambling joints—and was a short cut for delinquents and malingerers to join mobs. Its byproduct was jail, prison, rival factions at war, and mobster murders. The larger the city, the more concentrated the problems of liquor handling became.

The general populace held a critical view of the Volstead Act. It supposedly infringed on a man's freedom to do as he like, drink what he wanted and rule his life. The teen-age drinker felt he was coming of age when he got swacked and could show off.

Fishback Hill

Once upon a sunny day, in Oregon's lovely Oaken Way, there was a boy of a dozen seasons—a smart lad full of canny reasons.

Sez he, "What's weedy, and where's the cabbage?" He's a clever little savage!

O, he knew all right! But "ignorance is bliss." When fish are bitin', lads run-amiss!

Fluff clouds sail by; bees chant in clover—
    and Mitzie, his terrier, licks him all over.
There you lie upon the breaks,
    enjoying sounds a meadow makes.
In fields of yellow buttercups
    fat pollywogs insanely sup.

Iridescent tummies bravely glow,
    as wiggle-tails forever row.
There's no delay for such a day
    as Nature sets a grand array.
Cherries glow, apples shake—
    while strawberries grin beside a lake.

Join this kid with a lively hop. He loves strawberries with sugar a-top. Steals summer apples, juicy and fat. Rule is: I say, "Never pay Scat!" All boys are scoundrels—leave it at that!

* * *

In a town named Independence where oaks and orchards grow, we wandered in—all strangers—from Declo, Idaho.

A Normal School at Monmouth was the reason for our trip. My mother moved our family there for a short stay, while my father and older brother Roy continued to run the farm back in Declo, Idaho.

Independence, Oregon, had a branch of the busy Monmouth School. In the very heart of town was built a red brick school building. That is where I entered eighth grade, at IES, Independence Elementary School.

IES gym, constructed in 1926.

The homeroom teacher is Miss Thomas, a quaint old maid. I'll ne'er forget that sunny spot, set in a tree-lined glade. Our Principal greets "practice teachers"—students from nearby Independence Tech—as some Monmouth bus rolls in. Practice teachers strain their brains to teach their eighth-grade-kin.

In no time at all, my classmates learn to twit the Monmouth crowd. It is laughable! We have the upper hand as we read our sums out loud. The student teachers have *our* collars round *their* necks. We teach them more than they teach us. Weary, sometimes teary, they climb back on the bus.

They labor hard to entertain us, that they surely do! Toss us bones like you tempt a fuzzy dog. (As a once entranced eighth grader, I enjoyed this monologue.)

The students were a motley crew you would seldom see today. They came from fields and forest groves or depression bitten city coves.

Our class was unique. Two classmates were "late-bloomers." One eighteen year old "tap" was a pleasant chap—to Aitchey Sorg I doff my cap.

So many years have passed,
it's hard to treadle on.
I'm 92; It's blandly true:
the entire class is GONE!

Aitchey was nearly as old as some of those "practice teachers" from Monmouth's Oakish heights. He was our big brother—the chap who changed the lights. He did cut many didoes and pranks, but stayed 'round home at nights.

IES – Independence Elementary School.

The oldest girl in class was a maid named Hanna. She was late in graduating, but gentle as a Nanna. Missing school was common rule during the Big Depression. They were poor folks, probably, but, hey, I'm only guessin'.

The rest of our rill were run-'o-the-mill" tots of usual age. My teachers found I wuz unusual, a bit "above the average stage." I could read and spell like a goop from Pernell. My math was rather lean. Miss Thomas, I find, was very kind, and hesitant to demean, so I came up with better grades than I'd ever seen.

The practice teachers from Monmouth bleachers learned many truths in turn, like ways to pamper naughty lads who crave a yen to spurn. Kids don't like wordy dialogs or being pampered like some frogs. Prac-teachers taught me to do some sums and stopped my counting on my thumbs. In history class, we parked our objections—and with "Honest Abe" Lincoln made connections. Geography was better served, but math is where I badly curved. It's hard to drill those country boys who think multiplication's just annoys—not a bag of toys! We didn't fancy logarithms or mathy scams to arch our torsos toward Siam! In addition to sums, all teachers buy, add "B-sub-X" and "C-sub-Y"; interpolating mantissas of a logarithm, I don't get much entertainment with 'em! What a schism!

The Oregon landscape was full of mischief one hazy Autumn day. A breeze whispered to a lazy wren, "There's is no need to mimic men while birds have right of way!" The blackbird trills on a swinging stem. Every rippling stream hosts a flock of them. Wild flowers cast their scents *a-lea*. Rolling waves ripple in ecstasy!

Every breeze is a poem, loosely versed,
   in early June when trilliums burst.
There's a bluebird on the wing, a deer on the lea,
   as thunder rolls from sea to sea.

   The maple leaves whisper claims that providence never ceases. The busy ant did not listen—nor the bee—but the yellow butterfly, weaving on a meadow, assured each passer-by that drifting aimlessly, sipping nectar and storing none was the purpose of life. The maple-daughters plucked their brows and primped, sipping juleps from springs where meadows rouse. They entertained the grove with "boughs-in-sets and very merry pirouettes."

   A water dog rests where cresses lie. He had no watch; no dues to vie. A sparkling stream leapt through a wood. The salamander understood rain is pouring as matches flare. There'll be no fires in that tare. Wet matches are no good!

   The leader says, "Boys, zip up your gear—!"

   It was the best field trip of one entire year. Oregon raingear's very good—does a salamander, full of dander, still commandeer in Vitae's wood?

   Queen Anne's lace, pristine at first distraught-em, grew dustier and rustier each passive day of Autumn. Viewed from afar, the meadows are a phase of crazed summation where barefoot lads, with poles awry, are summoned by late summer sky. Summoned to a glade where, as a boy, I roamed and fished with hearty joy, headed nowhere of note, whistling through the woodland-mote of hazel bush and mistletoe, sights that only dreamers know, and barefoot boys with a roaming toe! Thorns, thistles and wasps were most "survivey" in glades of nettles and poison ivy—this is the heart of "girl-and-boy-land"; country kids just term it Joyland.

One lad walked with a wobbly limp, thistles tickled this barefoot-imp. Dame Nature smiled at the pasture gate, a clover-roving act of fate. The glad lad whistled to his waggy-tailed dog, by the name of Rover. They sat on a log.

"Lah-dee-dah," laddie sang across the hollow;
    flying swallows strove the grove to follow.
Blackbirds wheeled in fluttery rings
    to mark the path to Vitae Springs.

Blackberry vines, a bristly patch, had a snappy flavor home garden's won't match. In this drowsy landscape few predators roamed. Blithe breezes blew; bees honey-combed. There was no hawk to stalk the hill, no weasel prowled the merry rill; a day of butterflies-and-flowers, rippling wheat and bright sunflowers. Swallows rest, spiders pose; fuzzy caterpillars doze! Wild roses share these blessed stops in vales of vineyards, vines and hops.

All these wonders spun a strand of joys for pigtailed-girls and barefoot boys. What fun it is to stop a ferry or watch a pulley-race so merry! Waves rollick with those rolling cables, mid scents of musty woods and stables. I can't forget the Autumn's glow with water gurgling across-the-bow!

Hop season comes; what scents it brings. Maples are scarlet; smoke forms rings. A lazy haze surrounds the hill; great oaks change hue, nights are long and chill!

Willamette waves grow spunky; rain invades the cloud. Winter comes a little later. Here comes the hop yard crowd! They camp in every vineyard, reverberations oft' are loud! Dances start each evening; jazz really rules the crowd! Old folks "hit the sack." There are rites, fights and murder—most bad boys don't come back!

Big vineyards all have dryers; the odor's very keen. It is a money maker; the groves are tidy-clean. Homes are large and lovely. This country has a flair. The hop yards are big industry, a very grand affair.

Brother and I are picking hops; we find it is no snap! Our fingers soon get slivery. We don't like this rap! Hop baskets are so very big. Those hummers are quite tall. At picking potatoes we are good! Picking hops isn't fun at all!

This is picnic season, calm and serene, water ripples blue and clean. The stream is placid for the while. Willows and oaks have a lofty style. Blackbirds sing, frogs lie a'bed. No reptiles about; we've water dogs instead.

Salamander

or "Water Dog"

In a short time, threatening clouds may rise, as Willamette throws caution to the skies! Oregonians think, "Shucks, it's only RAIN!" But this river, on a rampage, will cause *a lot of pain*! It lays silt on hopfields, uproots mighty oaks, and swallows gravel bunkers with haughty, naughty strokes. It rolls across the lowlands, a vandal on the run. There are tons of devastation before the flooding's done!

When that river runs placidly, it's beauty warms our souls. We're captivated by it's power as toward Columbia it rolls!

One small farm kid from Idaho, who roamed those brushy hills, ne'er forgot Willamette's farmlands—the beauty of it's rills!

A Trip To Vitae Springs

They called it a Touring Model, a tourist-type two-seater. In other words—a sports car. I think it was blue, a light, airy tone; and there was ivory or cream striping across its tonneau. Strange how specific memories blur. Great expectations leapt in our hearts on first sight, and some of that joy still lingers in the memory of the prettiest car we ever owned.

I ought to know, I was the kid in overalls who sat in the back while my sisters warbled songs of the roaring twenties on the front seat with brother Luke. That older brother had a fine baritone voice until a high school teacher taught him to wobble. His voice was never as good after that. It was full of quivers and wavers. The year is 1923, the time of the Roaring Twenties; those roars are muted whimpers now.

Memories I can share are the smiling visage of a mother saddled with chores of cooking, sewing and laundry woes. Olga was poetic and artistic. She had little time to write prose or poetry; nevertheless, this is song she composed when we were small:

Lady moon, lady moon,
    where have you been?
When the sun is a king
    you could be queen;

But you roam in the night—
    all through the sky;
Lady moon! Lady moon!
    Please tell me why.

What a fine town Independence, Oregon, was, when touring cars sported isinglass curtains, made from fish bladders; a fact you're bound to doubt. As a boy, I loved clear summer evenings filled with stars when dusk brought a sense of mystery-and-mist. Under

scattered lamps, the moths swirled in didoes. Crickets murmured in the shadows of a modest house at "F" and Main Street.

Our neighbors were the Carpenters. Serene "Mama" Carpenter wore a perennial smile. Papa Carpenter was protective, watchful and rather detached from children's games. These busy parents saw their duty in the same way two robins figured their duty lay in a house with no roof in the front apple tree. Birds and people both pay a tax for settling down.

A fruitful life requires a mate, hatching progeny, fetching worms and helping hatchlings fly. Carpenters had three nestlings, two girls and a tot nicknamed "Brother." It was springtime. Robins in the apple tree disliked strangers, but I paid them scant attention.

Sissie, the oldest and sunniest girl would scamper up with her pigtails flying. "Come with me, Dwight, we're playing a game!"

Whatever the game was, we soon changed it—a time of innocent nonsense. They were wonderful playmates and Brother got his chance to join in. I was oldest and felt very comfortable playing court jester, magician or knave by turns.

Sometimes, Mrs. Carpenter brings lemonade and cookies. The hours fly south. Red leaves arrive. Hazel bushes in brushy sloughs close-by are loaded with promise. Oregon-scented, musty groves of oak and mistletoe create charming glades of bracken and briers where Queen Anne's lace simmers. Inevitable blackberry thickets scratch our ankles. That bumptuous, wild taste finds no match in cultivated gardens. Our lips fill with flavorsome seed, juice and delights.

> Wild blackberry and rambling rose,
> these are friends a wild boy knows!

The rains come. Bead frost festoons willows who proffer tinsel-like strings to light our way. Thus the morning fairies invite us to march down an arcade of frozen-jewelled teardrops—all the way to school.

It was an idyllic time, a year of awakening—a life of youthful promise, a "season of surprise."

That same year our first radio arrived. I helped father string the 100 foot antenna when he visited us on Christmas day. Freed-Eisemann was the name it bore. I still have the Rola speaker that stood near the set, tastefully designed on a slender tripod; the cone was about twelve inches circumference, and the central cone was of goatskin. These early sets were called TRFs (or tuned radio frequency receivers) and used number

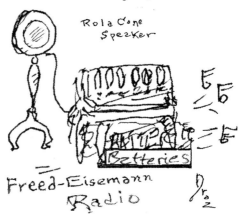

seventy-something Cunningham tubes for amplification, three gang tuning resistors with three large knobs to tune stations, and three types of batteries.

The year 1924 was the same year Independence, Oregon, opened the doors of I. T. S. Training School. A new school built of handsome red brick. Practice teachers from Monmouth Normal rode busses to Independence each day.

That winter a flood, racing down the Willamette River, wiped out a gravel bunker at the edge of town and carried 30 houses from Eugene with the rest of the flotsam.

Hike To Vitae Springs

That same year a crippled lad, a sandy haired, lanky lad, nicknamed Giraffe, and a passel of other schoolboys from Sunday School, boarded the ferry for a hike to Vitae Springs. It rained most of the way. On the river path, odors of ferns and moss mingled with the musk of trampled leaves along with patters of misty rain; spongy mud squished underfoot. This sounds dismal enough, but Oregonians dress for rain and think jolly little about it.

We tramped through groves of oak with mistletoe'd tops down a path that didn't care if it went anywhere, and we eventually arrived at the spring, none the worse for gravy-gray sky.

I'd never seen a water dog, and there it was, paddling in the brimming spring. What fairy creatures, that rusting tummy looks antique and bodacious. Each of us held it a time—a miniature bit of dragon stuff—a typical Oregon hike. We squatted by the spring with cool rain slopping on yellow slickers.

Oregon air has that earthy flavor; it fills your lungs. The chest swells tight! You spread your arms and shout for no reason—or is it done because you're a boy? You plan to

accomplish nothing, you make a point of destroying anything that looks symmetrical. Rocks are always useful to destroy symmetry. You lob them in ponds, rout game birds, pepper them at squirrels.

Comes a pause—you can always day dream— pretend you're pirate or captain, jewel thief or emperor.

There must be a treasure somewhere near!

It's a typical hike, squatted by a spring munching a sandwich and sipping hot cocoa. Back across Oregon woodland we tack. I don't even remember where Vitae Springs lies as I mull this memory now.

One thing I do remember: the contrast of that day to the same day one year before on a farm in Idaho. Boys about that age believe life continues forever—you doubt you'll grow much bigger. Some school boys, myself for one, figured we'd fail to pass an achievement test at year's end—but no matter. The world was wide. Grownups were the cause of all our troubles. I had no idea why they were in charge of us. They just were.

Big Brothers

Big brothers came and went like shadows. You tolerated them, but, they weren't seemingly related, though living in the same house, doing things you couldn't do. My brothers had watches and other perks. One had an Indian motorcycle, they had first pick of saddle horses and the best saddles. I usually rode the red mare bareback. She'd been a buggy horse, was slowing down and had a hard trot. Granted, she was the safest horse.

Those brothers seldom played with me. God forbid! My life and aims were a child's. We were years apart.

Each day, those brothers announced what you could and *should not* do. "Don't play with my twenty-two automatic!" Roy warned. I checked it out—and shot a hole through the bedroom floor. "Don't ever wear my Stetson," said brother Luke; so I tried that gem, but it wouldn't fit. I didn't expect any good strokes from either of 'em. In effect, their message was:

"You're a problem—just go away. You're a spoiled monster—get lost. Why must you bother me? I've a date—don't hang around us. And, by the way, mama needs stove wood—get it! Milk the cow with the little spigots, my hands are too big. Papa wants water in the kitchen." That's a partial summation of their "friendly" memos.

Life's Hard Tasks

"The horses need more water, too. You can pump it; don't complain," some older voice intones. Did you ever see how much water just two horses can guzzle? It makes me groan even yet to think of straining my backbone on that creaky, sneaky pump.

"Fetch me another bucket full, son," says pop.

"l need some wood right now!" mama exclaims.

The ax was at the block. The wood pile was dismal as a cemetery to me—always threatening any fun.

You were usually nursing a blister some place. Torture on end—take it away! Never live in a house with two brothers—seven and ten years older. They're a generation away. Were they ever nice? Seldom. Are they gone? Yes! Do you miss them? I suppose. There were times they helped me, a little, in later years, but did they share fun and games? Practically never.

I was on my own.

Back to Oregon: I had friends my age to play with. Thank God there were things like waterdogs, and blackbirds to chase. I loved that wet, dripping hike to Vitae Springs with no brother to say, "Nay." Some playmates were bigger than I, but they weren't my relation; that made a world of difference. Some were freckled, some were fat; some weren't as strong as I—in spite of the pesky limp—that paining joint!

Can Hockey

How we loved to play can hockey, using a hazelnut limb. You sacked a slough and broke some branches. Start the game, man the clubs:
"Hockey one!" Strike clubs.
"Hockey two!" Strike clubs again.
"Hockey three!" And WHAM!—strike the can.
Up and down the street you sped, chasing condensed milk cans with Sego, or Carnation labels, nobly designed for hockey games. Pouring milk from these marvelous tins at breakfast was incidental. By afternoon the empty wonders were hockey pucks. You yelled, jostled and whacked. Great fun!

A staunch can lasted three games. By then, it was a blob of smashed metal with solder clinging, and labels flapping. It came from a garbage can, arced into the sky a time, and then—beaten, stomped and trampled—back to trash it went.

Hockey gear cost us nothing. A wise choice for lads without credit. Hazel sticks cost "zilch-wilch." For that matter, we didn't pay anything for most of the fun in those days.

An Auto Made Of Laths

Back in Idaho, my playmates made fancy cars from scraps. They didn't have wheels, just pretend. Three old laths nailed together made the body. One nail, bent over, was a spark lever; the other was for gas.

(Model "T"s had these two levers perched under the steering wheel.) We used roofing tacks to simulate horn buttons. You held this simple frame with one hand and added a passenger to keep things steadier.

The contraption was similar to earlier play like riding a stick horse. You really did all the work. Just keep things hopping; don't get snagged in the brush pile; keep things light-hearted. Drive this with

imagination! That's a cardinal rule. You skidded to a stop for anyone thumbing a ride on that lath framed Cadillac. It was great fun pretending to stop for gas, oil and water.

Now it's time to start 'er up: you sputter a time, yanking at the choke, purr as the motor "warms." O, there are many fine noises involved at start up. Now you throw this behemoth in gear, the frame is waist high; you shift into a trot and roar up the speedway. Of course, there's no engine, no seats and no wheels—but the sound effects are great. The passengers had better keep up.

"Now, hit the brakes!" someone yells. "Watch fer collision!"

In earlier days at Cotterel, Luke's "lath cars" lasted pretty well until he grew careless. He'd grab a hammer and make repairs. If it fell apart, you could always walk home. There was no gas crisis, but you claimed you ran out. Punctures were apt to be thistles in the foot. My sisters wound up driving Luke's junkers.

Huckleberry Days

Enough of that fantasy. We are back to those times poets term the Huckleberry Days. In Idaho, cherries and apples tempted us—just over a fence along some canal. Cherries were meant for pirating boys and robins; in the main, fruit was free. Oregon blackberries were choicest of all, glistening clusters of swollen globes—what a flavor!

There were other activities not connected to the stomach, of course. You went fishing at *the Drop*, searched ponds for water skippers (quick-footed as dancing dervishes.) Dragonfly nymphs looked horrible; we captured 'em to petrify snooping girls.

Dimes were big time. A quarter made young

eyes glitter. A silver dollar was awesome. Our riches were, in the main, open skies, clouds to track—always drifting eastward in that buffeting wind. We heard pheasants crowing, frogs chanting in march rhythms.

So...who needs money? In the final analysis, we did.

Boys loved to play marble games involving crockies, dobabes, limeys and taws.[13] You needed plenty of money to buy 'em—that's how it was. I bought most of mine at the Woolworth store.

There were natty city-pretties clerking in the five-and-dime. It's a frame for "marble capers" at apple blossom time! New temptations caught my eye, all along the painted wall hung tasty twists of licorice prized by country boys et'all!

Classy candy counters held a fabled Caliph's dream. Inside two toothy cages candy canes in clusters gleam!

Chocolate bars participated,
           our hungry ivories growled.
Then, our dimes evaporated;
           so, we sighed, extricated,
                      and absconded through the door.

Oregon woods were somehow bonny even in that streaming rain. We're headin' out for brimming springs on a rainy winter day. (One old man still remembers, eighty-six years just slipped away.)

---

[13] There were numerous names common to the 1920s. Taws were the marbles you shot to bounce others out of the ring. Dobabes, crockies, and limeys were among the ones you intended to capture.

And here's a funny little chap
    in a pool, taking a nap.
Fare-the-well, my rustic friend.
      nestled in those foamy rings.
This world is full
    of wonderful things;
Like a tiny "water dog"
    in the rills of Vitae Springs.

"Green Mountain" by Dwight R. Droz

Sketch of the author at 92 by his son Dennis Droz,
February 2005 (drawn in three and a half minutes).

Printed in the United States
29138LVS00002B/1-99

9 780970 635754